My Father's House

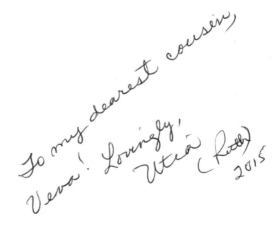

To my dearest cousin,
Vera! Lovingly,
Utca (Ruth)
2015

My Father's House

By Ruth Deyneka Erdel

Copyright © 2015 Slavic Gospel Association
6151 Commonwealth Drive
Loves Park, Illinois 61111

Printed in USA

ISBN 978-1-56773-127-9

Special thanks to Barbara Whitfield who drew the
sketches for this publication.

Table of Contents

Chapter 1

How It All Began 7

Chapter 2

Jack and Ruth in Ministry 23

Chapter 3

Journeys to the CIS 35

Chapter 4

The Tabernacle 45

Chapter 5

The Gate 53

Chapter 6

The Brazen Altar 59

Chapter 7

The Laver 69

Chapter 8

The Table of the Bread of the Presence 79

Chapter 9

The Lampstand 95

Chapter 10

The Altar of Incense 121

Chapter 11

The Holy of Holies 139

Chapter 12

Our Heavenly Home 147

Epilogue 155

Chapter 1

How It All Began

It all began in the small village of Staramlynia in Belarus. A great celebration was being held in the yellow house down the dirt road. One of the village's young women, Anastasia Deyneka, had given birth to a baby boy! It was July 12, 1898, Saint Peter's Day, so the parents named their new son Peter Nahumovich Deyneka!

Nahum and Anastasia Deyneka were poor. They had only limited land to raise their cabbages and potatoes. Other babies continued to arrive, and it seemed that the one room hut became smaller and smaller. Nahum had to spend a lot of his time fishing in the nearby Yaselda River in order to support his family. How young Peter loved to go fishing with his father! Many times they stayed on the river all day and all night if they were not catching many fish.

One summer Peter was sent to a small island a few kilometers away from his home to herd cattle. There were wild wolves prowling about. He kept a fire going all night, hugging his little dog, as he carefully watched the cattle. At times his sisters would visit him, bringing him fresh bread. They would tease Peter about perhaps going to America someday to make money to help the family. Then they could have a better life with something more than soup to eat. Their family was often hungry.

One evening after their supper Peter's papa said to him, "Petiya, I must tell you that in the village men are talking about the parents who have sent their sons across the ocean to work. Dollars are coming back from them, and this is helping their families. My dear son," said his papa with a tremor in his voice, "with several children now, Mama and I have decided to send you to America to help us."

Peter was stunned. Leave home? Leave his village? Leave his family to go to a land far across the ocean where he did not know the language? His heart was pounding, and his throat went dry. He wanted to cry out a loud "No!" But in the light of the burning candle, Peter saw tears running down his papa's cheeks. He knew that he must say "Yes!" He loved his papa. He loved his mama. And, oh, how he loved his two sisters, Tekla and Anastasia, and his little brothers. He would go! He would try to be brave. After all, he was almost 16 years of age.

Money was borrowed for the transportation. His mama cried while she carefully packed his things. On March 3, 1914, friends and family gathered for their farewells. As they walked down the road, the neighbors came out of their homes to wish him well. Amidst sobs and weeping, Peter looked back at his papa's house. Would he ever see his home again? Then he climbed aboard an open wagon. "Petiya, when are you coming back?" cried his brothers and sisters, waving frantically. "I will send help soon," he shouted. "I promise! I promise!"

And with a "click" to the horse, the wagon slowly moved down the road.

As his papa drove the twenty five kilometers to the railway station, his heart was heavy with grief at the thought of separation from his oldest son. He told Peter that he was sorry that he had asked him to go to America. But now it was too late, too late to change plans. When the noisy train, spouting smoke and steam, arrived about two A.M., Peter grabbed his papa and hugged him with fear. He had never seen a train before. It looked so huge and so powerful! After a gripping embrace, Peter climbed aboard, blinded with tears. Would he ever see his papa again? The train pulled away slowly, and Peter kept crying.

Young Peter Deyneka

Some three weeks later, first buffeted by travel on slow trains through Eastern Europe, then by a rough steerage passage across the North Sea and the Atlantic Ocean, and finally by train in America (where he understood nothing), young Peter arrived at his destination- his cousin Walter's door in the city of Chicago, Illinois.

Almost at once he began walking the streets, looking for work. He took whatever jobs he could find and faithfully sent money home. Lonely and discouraged, he usually spent Sundays just walking and walking. One Sunday he was startled to hear Russian music coming from across the street. Several men were singing. He loved music. He stopped to listen. This was followed by some "religious lectures." The lectures did not interest him, but his heart responded to the melodious sounds of the Russian language. He returned the following Sunday to hear more and stood a bit closer. Week after week these Russian men testified about the love of Christ, and Peter kept returning. They explained how God had sent His Son, Jesus, to die on the cross, shedding His blood to pay for the sins of people on earth.

This was the first time Peter had ever heard the Gospel. He actually tried to argue with these men. They, in turn, invited him to join them for home-cooked meals. He enjoyed that! They gave him a New Testament and encouraged him to attend English-speaking churches, explaining that by doing so he would learn better English. He took their suggestion. On Sundays he would attend both his friends' Russian meetings as well as English services at Moody Church. He heard wonderful gospel preaching in both services. Many months passed before he completely understood the Gospel. Finally, on January 18, 1920, deeply convicted of his sins, he went to the altar at Moody Church and received Jesus as His personal Savior. That was the turning point of his life!

Another very memorable day for Peter was July 25, 1920. On that beautiful sunny day he was baptized at nearby Cedar Lake Bible Conference in Indiana. In his testimony he said, "How I thank God for the privilege of accepting His Son and for being buried with Him in baptism!"

By now Peter was motivated by the verse in Matthew 28:19 which says, *Go therefore and make disciples of all the nations, baptizing them in the name of the Father and the Son and the Holy Spirit!* After his conversion he was finding great joy in telling other people that God loved them.

About this time Paul Rader, the pastor of Moody Church, returned from a round-the-world missionary trip. In every country where he had visited, he saw the need for missionaries. When Pastor Rader returned to his church in Chicago, he challenged his young people to surrender their lives to God and to be willing to go and spread His Word. Peter's own heart was touched. He remembered his own teen years when he first came to America. How desolate and how distraught he had been without Christ. His heart had cried out with the

Psalmist who said, *Look to the right and see; for there is no one who regards me; there is no escape for me; NO ONE CARES FOR MY SOUL* (Psalm 142:4).

In another evening service Pastor Rader was calling for youth to fully surrender their lives to God. In his sermon he said, "Come, dedicate your life to serve the Lord." Just then the choir began singing the hymn: "I'll Go Where You Want Me to Go Dear Lord."

While the choir was still singing, Peter went forward and fell on his knees. With tears he told the Lord that he was willing to be what God wanted him to be. Oh, yes, he would go wherever the Lord wanted him to go! He was ready to consecrate his life to Christ and become a missionary. Yes, he would take the light of Jesus to his own Russian-speaking people and to others. He would serve Christ with all of his heart!

I'll Go Where You Want Me To Go

It may not be on the mountain height
Or over the stormy sea,
It may not be at the battle's front
My Lord will have need of me.
But if, by a still, small voice He calls
To paths that I do not know,
I'll answer, dear Lord, with my hand in thine:
I'll go where you want me to go.

(Chorus)
I'll go where you want me to go, dear Lord,
Over mountain or plain or sea;
I'll say what you want me to say, dear Lord;
I'll be what you want me to be.

Perhaps today there are loving words
Which Jesus would have me speak;
There may be now in the paths of sin
Some wand'rer whom I should seek.
O Savior, if Thou wilt be my guide,
Tho dark and rugged the way,
My voice shall echo the message sweet:
I'll say what you want me to say.

There's surely somewhere a lowly place
In earth's harvest fields so wide
Where I may labor through life's short day
For Jesus, the Crucified.
So trusting my all to Thy tender care,
And knowing Thou lovest me,
I'll do Thy will with a heart sincere:
I'll be what You want me to be.

Eager to learn more of God's Word and to prepare himself to serve the Lord, he began attending evening classes at the Moody Bible Institute. A few months later the way opened for him to attend a Christian and Missionary Alliance Bible School in Minnesota as a full-time student. There the students were very kind to him. They often spent hours helping him understand his lessons better, since he was limited in the English language.

But his limited English never stopped him from witnessing for Christ. His earnest, daily prayer was that God would make him a real soul-winner. He was often moved by what Jesus told his disciples, *Follow me, and I will make you fishers of men* (Matthew 4:19). He would recall those memorable times when he went fishing with his father back home on the Yaselda River in his Belarus homeland. But now fishing for the souls of men gave him an even deeper joy.

After graduating from Bible School in 1924, Peter continued to witness for the Lord. For a while he served as a pastor in a small country church. However, he was sad because World War I had severed all communication with his family in Belarus. He had not heard from them for several years. Finally he received a letter from his mama. "My dear son, we are starving! First your brothers Vasili, Maksim, and Ivan died of starvation. I could not find enough food to cook in the soup and only added grass. And your sisters Tekla and Anastasia also died. Only your brother Andrei, Papa, and I are still alive, but we are very weak. Please come and help us. Come!"

Peter was devastated! His loved ones had died. And they had died without Christ! He could not eat or sleep. He spent the next day and night in prayer. His heart was broken! He needed to send them money immediately. But he did not have any. He took his burden to the Lord, crying, praying, and asking God for help.

While reading the Scriptures he read, *Do not let your heart be troubled; believe in God, believe also in Me* (John 14:1). *If you ask Me anything in My name, I will do it* (John 14:14). He kept praying and praying.

Not long after this, a friend of his came to see him. "My dear brother Peter, I have had such a burden for you during the past two days," he said. "The Lord has laid it on my heart to give you $50.00. Maybe you have friends or relatives in Russia who are in need."

"Oh, thank you, thank you," said Peter. "Praise the Lord!"

With deep gratitude he immediately cabled the money to his mama and papa. God had answered his prayer. Now he knew that there would be bread on his parents' table once again.

With communication established once more, Peter wrote long letters to his parents and to his brother Andrei, explaining the way of salvation to them. He sent them tracts and a New Testament. He begged them to pray and to open their hearts to the Lord. His father began to read the Word of God, but in his letters to Peter he kept asking him: "Oh, dear son, please tell me more about 'life after death.'"

This was all so new to him.

By now Peter's heart was focused on his homeland. World War I had ended. He must return to his people to preach the Gospel. But where were the funds for travel expenses? Where was money to purchase Scriptures to take along for his family and friends back in Belarus?

He began to pray. He asked his friends to pray. *And my God will supply all your needs according to His riches in glory by Christ Jesus* (Philippians 4:19), was a verse he often quoted! Praise the Lord, once again God answered prayer! Many friends helped him. On October 1, 1925, he sailed for Europe, so excited that the two weeks of travel seemed only a blur.

Upon arriving in Belarus, he rented a horse and wagon. Finally he arrived in Homsk, the small town near his village, on a market day. Some villagers recognized him and hurried to find his mother and brother. They brought them to the wagon. After eleven and one-half years, mother and son fell into a loving embrace. Peter tried to talk to his Mother, but she kept crying. Finally, in a broken voice she said, "Oh, Pietya...if...only... you...had...come...sooner...Papa died...only...five...weeks ago."

Now Peter began to sob. He laid his head on the horse's neck and sobbed. He had come home with such anticipation to see his Papa, but he was too late. Too late to see him face to face. Too late to tell him more about Jesus and His love. He had come too late to tell him about life after death. Oh, how Peter cried. He was too late! Too late!

Full of emotion, he lifted his head. With his eyes wet with tears, he suddenly noticed his younger brother Andrei standing silently on the side and quickly embraced him. Together, mother, brother, and Peter traveled the short distance to their village of Staramlynia. As soon as he saw his father's house his eyes filled with tears. His Papa was gone!

Soon even the neighbors followed him right into his family's hut. "Petro, tell us about America. Tell us of all the riches and gold you found there."

He didn't even have time to take off his jacket. People pressed him with their questions. There was confusion, and he was tired. But he began by telling them how he had found the greatest gift in the world. In America he had found the Lord as his personal Savior! Day after day people kept coming into their house. "Tell us more. We never heard anything like this before. Tell us more from the Bible," they would say.

And Peter kept preaching to them. His own boyhood home had become a House of Prayer.

Before long he was going from village to village, preaching the Gospel. People walked for miles to attend his services. Many prayed and repented of their sins. It was while he was preaching in one of the villages that he met Vera, a sweet, lovely young lady who had accepted the Lord three years earlier. People told him that she loved to pray. They told him that she faithfully attended their Sunday services even though her parents disapproved.

To reach the church on time, she had to walk through a forest in the dark, early-morning hours. She ran through the woods barefoot, carrying her shoes under her arm. She would be so frightened of wolves, that upon entering the woods, she would start singing as loud as she could and run as fast as possible. Often she slipped and fell on the muddy trail. But she kept going.

Soon Peter and Vera began to pray together about their relationship. Both felt that the Lord had brought them together. Several months later, on May 23, 1926, they were married in the town of Homsk in Belarus. Ministering together, Vera would sing hymns with her beautiful soprano voice, and Peter would preach. Souls were saved and people were encouraged.

Some of the area preachers who had joined with Peter in his evangelistic endeavor began to encourage him to return to the United States in order to raise funds for their ministry. They needed more Bibles and books, as well as bicycles to help with their travel between villages. Since Peter knew English, they suggested that he return to America to see if his friends there would be able to help them.

His bride Vera had to remain in the village with his mother until all the proper papers for her immigration to the United States could be secured, and her ticket could be purchased. After a tearful farewell, Peter returned to the United States in August 1926. He stayed in New York City to arrange for Vera's necessary papers for immigration and to await her arrival.

While in New York City, Peter met Rev. Ivan Stepanovich Prokhanoff. He was a leading Russian-evangelical statesman from Leningrad who had come to New York to raise funds to print Russian Christian literature. The supply of Bibles in Russia had been exhausted. Miraculously, Prokhanoff had received permission from the government in Leningrad to print Bibles and song books. Some peasants were even offering a cow or a sack of grain for one Bible.

Upon meeting Peter, brother Prokhanoff saw his zeal and his desire to serve the Lord. He invited Peter to join his organization. He assigned Peter the project of raising funds for printing Russian Bibles, as well as for funds to print song books and Christian magazines. Peter traveled and preached in many churches. His heart overflowed with joy as souls came to the Lord, and funds were raised for the printing as well.

It was December 8, 1926. Peter was standing on the New York dock, anxiously watching his wife's ship come sailing in. He had been blessed in his ministry in America for the past months, but, oh, how he had missed his wife! At last she came down the gang plank. How happy they were to be together again! Soon they traveled by train to Chicago, Illinois, where they established their new home in a small rented apartment. Peter enthusiastically continued his ministry with Ivan Prokhanoff's organization.

Vera was especially happy to find a wonderful Russian Evangelical Christian Church in Chicago. She loved to sing in the choir. She participated in the ladies' prayer gatherings. There were many Russian immigrants like her, and she appreciated their fellowship while Peter continued his extensive travels.

Peter was invited to minister in both Russian and English-speaking churches across the United States and Canada. He preached at Bible conferences and in young people's meetings as well. Everywhere people repented of their sins. Others dedicated their lives to serve Christ. With the Lord's help, money was raised to print thousands of Russian Bibles and hymnbooks, as well as for support for Slavic pastors.

In March 1928, an invitation came for Peter to preach in South Dakota. He was hesitant to accept the invitation because Vera was expecting their first child. However, his wife urged him to go. She was confident that God would take care of her and their baby. Peter left reluctantly, but he arranged that their relative, Julia, who was living with them, would send a telegram as soon as the baby was born.

And so it was that on Thursday, March 29, 1928, Vera gave birth to a very tiny baby girl. Julia hurried to send the telegram to South Dakota. "Baby girl born on March 29. Vera and baby are well!"

Peter was thrilled. He immediately got on his knees and thanked the Lord that all had gone well. "What will you name your little daughter?" asked his friends. "I don't know," said Peter. "We only talked about having a boy whose name would be Peter. We never mentioned a girl's name."

After the evening service Peter and his host family gathered around the kitchen table. Peter took his Bible, prayed, and asked the Lord for the right name for his daughter. He leafed through his Bible. His eye caught the book of Ruth. He stopped. "Ruth! Yes, Ruth! Ruth in the Bible, who left her sinful nation and accepted the true God. Yes, we shall name our little daughter, Ruth. And we will pray that she, too, will follow the Lord and do His will. And we will pray that she will also help others even as Ruth did in the Bible."

And so it was that I (who write this) became Ruth Petrovna Deyneka, daughter of Vera Ivanovna and Peter Nahumovich Deyneka.

I was born into a wonderful home where everything was done by PRAYER! My Mama and my Papa were praying people. Papa continued his preaching ministry. His heart constantly yearned to take the Gospel to his Slavic people. My dearest Mama was his greatest encourager and greatest prayer partner. In 1930 he was invited to take his second missionary journey to Europe. Once again he prayed, and once again the Lord supplied all of his needs. On February 22, 1930, Papa sailed from New York to England. After services in London, he traveled on to preach in Berlin, Belgium, Latvia, Estonia, and Poland.

With his heart beating fast, on March 22, 1930, Papa finally arrived at his birthplace, the village of Staramlynia. His eyes eagerly searched for his family's yellow house down the road! Then he saw it. And there was his mother standing by the window. When she saw the horse and wagon coming down the road, she jumped up and ran outside, past the picket fence, and fell on her son's neck. She cried out, "Petiya, Petiya, I just gave my heart to Jesus. He has made me a new person."

What overwhelming joy flooded over my Father. His precious Mama had just accepted the Lord! Again, God had answered his prayers!

For several weeks he traveled to neighboring towns and villages, sharing the Gospel. People walked from the surrounding hamlets to attend the services. Many opened their hearts to Christ. Many repented. Many were baptized. And always, there was the deep joy of now being able to pray and to fellowship with his own precious Mama. He cherished every moment with her. There were many tears the day he kissed his mother good-bye, but his heart rejoiced that now she had become a child of God!

Returning to Chicago in June 1930, he continued in ministry with Ivan Stepanovich Prokhanoff until June 1931. Then in July 1931, Pastor Paul Rader, under whose preaching my Papa had been saved, called him to lead the Russian ministry of Rader's missionary organization. Papa was humbled to be able to work together with the man who had brought him to Christ. He participated in large conferences with Paul Rader. He led many prayer meetings and preached in many churches.

In September 1933, Papa received a cablegram inviting him to speak at a special conference in Poland. Upon his arrival, people walked as far as forty kilometers to attend that conference. It lasted nearly five hours. Papa's heart was moved with compassion to see their spiritual hunger. Many found the Lord, and Christians were revived.

During those days of evangelism, he was asked to be a delegate from the Slavic churches in Poland to a large conference to be held in Sweden. Papa agreed to represent them.

Upon reaching Sweden, he was overwhelmed by the beauty of that country with its many little islands. But what really amazed him was to find several Swedish pastors and workers who had learned to speak Russian well. They were endeavoring to reach their Russian neighbors with the Gospel. Papa was very impressed by their zeal. In turn, they encouraged him to launch out and do something even more substantial for his own Slavic people. Returning to America with this new vision, Papa shared it with Mama. Together they began to spend time in fasting and prayer. What did God have for them in the future?

After much prayer, Papa met with Pastor Paul Rood, a Swedish minister in the city of Chicago. Papa shared his vision of founding a mission to Slavic peoples. Pastor Rood strongly encouraged him to do this. Papa then contacted several other Christian leaders. They, too, expressed deep interest in his vision. These men gave him counsel and promised to help him. So it was that one bitterly-cold winter afternoon, this group of men (who became his committee) joined my father for a very special prayer meeting. That same day, January 6, 1934, by God's grace, the SLAVIC GOSPEL ASSOCIATION WAS BORN THROUGH PRAYER!

Life in America

All this time, although I was born in America, I was being brought up like a little girl in Russia. Our Mama cooked the best borscht, vareniki, guloptzi, holodetz, kapusta, blini, and oh, so many other delicious Russian foods. Before I started to attend school, Mama began to teach me to read and write in the Russian language. When I actually started school, I did not speak any English. But fortunately, I learned it quickly. My Mama sent me off to school dressed like a typical Russian girl, with big bows at the end of my braids and wearing long skirts and heavy stockings. She also made sure that all three of her children took piano lessons. My brother Peter, sister Lydia, and I loved attending the Russian Evangelical Christian Church on Crystal Street in Chicago, where most of the services were held in the Russian language.

Sometimes when I was a little girl, I was sad because Papa was gone from home so often. I recall one evening as we were

Peter, Ruth, and Vera Deyneka

getting ready for bed, I asked my mama, "Oh, why does Papa go on so many trips? He is hardly ever home, and I miss him."

She explained that because Papa loved Jesus so much, he wanted other people to love Him, too, especially our Russian-speaking people. She looked at the clock and said, "Look, it is almost time for Papa to be preaching right now. Let's pray and ask Jesus to help him. Let's pray that someone will accept Christ into his heart this very night."

Mama called my brother and sister. Together we read some Scripture verses, as was our nightly custom. Then the four of us knelt together by our parents' bed. Mama prayed first, and the three of us children followed her. She thanked the Lord for the privilege that our Papa had to tell others about Christ. Mama's prayers, loving explanations, and kisses brought us peace and understanding. We loved our parents.

Day after day Mama and Papa faithfully taught us children to love and to honor the Lord. They explained to us that we needed to accept Jesus into our hearts as our own personal Savior. Above our small kitchen table hung a plaque which I read every day. It said:

SAY nothing you would not want Jesus to hear!

DO nothing you would not want Jesus to see!

GO nowhere that Jesus would not go with you!

And then there came a day which I shall never forget. It was the day that I knelt and prayed with both Mama and Papa by my side! I repented of my sins. Then I asked Jesus to forgive me, to cleanse me, and to come into my heart. All this happened soon after I celebrated my ninth birthday. I was happy that I was nine years of age and even more happy that I now had a "spiritual" birthday, also.

I often saw my parents on their knees, praying! They often spoke to us children about their burden for people without Christ. From them, we learned our own responsibility to give a witness for the Lord.

They also taught us to love our Slavic heritage. We always spoke to them in the Russian language. I am in full agreement with the verse in Psalm 16:6 where David said, *The lines have fallen to me in pleasant places; Indeed, my heritage is beautiful to me.*

Ruth at age four and a half, with her parents and Peter Jr.

Two very important events took place in my life when I was thirteen years old. In April 1941, Papa returned home from South America where he had spent over five months preaching in Argentina, Uruguay, Paraguay, Chile, Ecuador, and Cuba. Soon he was invited to give a report about this trip at the Russian-Evangelical Crystal Street Church in Chicago. What a report! He told how hundreds of Russian-speaking people across South America had gone to the altar weeping and had repented of their sins. He also told us that missionaries were needed to witness to the many others who were still without Christ. "Who will be willing to give his life to serve the Lord as a missionary to them?" he asked. "Who will say 'yes' to Jesus?" That question touched my young heart.

Hearing that challenge, I remembered that my own aunties and uncles, whom I had never met, had died in Belarus without Jesus. They had never heard about the Lord and His love for them. Yes, I wanted to tell others about Him. I wanted to dedicate my life to God! I almost ran to the front of the church and knelt in prayer. With deep emotion and many tears, I prayed and committed my life to Christ. Yes, I wanted to serve God and be a missionary. From that moment on, when anyone asked me about my future, my response was simply, "I am going to be a Russian missionary someday if that is God's will."

Three months later I took my first step towards that goal. I was baptized in Lake Michigan with thirty other young people from our Crystal Street Church. It was a great day of celebration for all of us!

Chapter 2

Jack and Ruth in Ministry

~~~~~~⁓⁓⁓⁓/𝕁\⁓⁓⁓⁓~~~~~~

The happiest day of my life was July 7, 1950. *That was the day I left for the mission field!* It was the day I had so long anticipated, so long prayed for, so long imagined. I was twenty-two years of age.

A few weeks before this, I had graduated from a Christian university. Almost at once the Lord opened a door for me to go to Europe as a missionary! There I joined Rose Kucher, a Ukrainian-Canadian SGA missionary in Frankfort, Germany. Rose had already been working in Europe as a missionary among Slavic refugees for a year. I found her a wonderful coworker.

Together Rose and I ministered to Slavic refugees who had been placed in camps in the Frankfurt area. There they were waiting to be assigned sponsors in Canada, the United States, Brazil, Venezuela, Australia, and elsewhere. Most of these refugees had heard little about God or the Bible. We found great joy in telling them about Jesus and His love.

We held women's and children's meetings during the week in different camps. My father had bought me a small accordion, and I played it as we sang choruses and hymns. Always we opened God's Word. There was rejoicing when refugees trusted the Lord as their Savior.

On a memorable afternoon following one such service, I noticed a man waiting to speak to us after the meeting. As I greeted him, he said, "Pardon, me. I have a question for you. The book you ladies were reading from today, how new is it?"

I was startled by his question.

I said, "The Bible is an old book. It has been translated into the Russian language for many years."

Then he asked me, "So why is this the first time that I have heard of such a book?"

I stood there looking at his inquisitive gaze. To think, God had sent Rose and me to Frankfurt, Germany, to introduce this man to the Bible, and to show him and others like him the way to Jesus. How I thanked the Lord for the privilege of being a missionary!

It was during our time of ministry to these refugees that Rose and I met our future husbands. Both of these young men were also missionaries to Europe, and the Lord brought us all together.

Rose married my cousin, Nicolai Pavlovich Leonovich, who had been born in Belarus. After their marriage they became radio missionaries, first broadcasting over Trans World Radio in Tangier, Africa, and then in Monaco for many years. Eventually they returned to the United States, where they continued in faithful service to the Lord both in America and in the former Soviet Union. Nicolai died unexpectedly on a ministry trip while in Irpen, Ukraine, on May 23, 2013.

After ministering in Europe for almost three years, I married Jacob Ivanovich Shalanko, a Canadian-Russian missionary who had been preaching in a refugee camp in Trieste, Italy. After our marriage, Slavic Gospel Association sent us to radio station Voice of the Andes in Quito, Ecuador, South America, to be radio missionaries. We arrived there on December 24, 1954. For nearly 30 years we sang and preached the Gospel from Voice of the Andes to Russian-speaking people in 87 countries around the world.

Peter and Vera Deyneka (in front) with the SGA Russian radio team at HCJB in 1956: (left to right) Const and Elizabeth Lewshenia, Stella Jarema, Helen Zernov, and Ruth and Jack Shalanko.

How we appreciated ministering together in Quito with Constantine and Elizabeth Lewshenia, as well as with Helen Zernov. In later years, our beautiful Canadian-Ukrainian soprano singer, Stella Jarema, joined the Voice of the Andes staff, as did also Andres and Elena Ralek of Paraguay and Argentina, Alex and Elodia Kuvshinikov of Russia and Argentina, and Wally and Natasha Kulakoff of Australia. What a wonderful team!

We also learned the Spanish language, and Jack was soon invited to preach among Spanish churches. We sang duets together, with Jack accompanying on his guitar and I on my accordion. Eventually, Jack preached throughout Ecuador as well as in Peru, Colombia, Argentina, Paraguay, Venezuela, Uruguay, and Brazil, speaking in English, Russian and Spanish.

There were two very memorable episodes of my husband Jack's life that I would like to mention. In January 1956, five outstanding American missionaries bonded together to take the Gospel to the fierce Auca (Waodani) Indian tribe in Ecuador. Instead of a friendly meeting which these missionaries were expecting, they were brutally killed by those same Indians.

Jack was asked to be part of a rescue party composed of seven missionaries as well as soldiers and Indian guides. They traveled by canoe on the Curaray River to the beach where the men had camped and where the attack had occurred. There they found the bodies of the missionary men in the river. Jack helped as the rescue party buried them on the same sandy beach where they had lost their lives by Auca spears. Jack was deeply moved by their martyrdom. They had been our personal friends.

Then in December 1968, our family was invited to visit the friendly Secoya Indians, who were living in the Ecuadorian jungle. Mary and Orville Johnson and their four children, American missionaries with the Wycliffe Bible Translators, had gone to live in a Secoya village. After they had learned the Secoya language, they began the arduous task of translating the New Testament into that tongue.

After twelve years, several Secoyas had repented of their sins and requested baptism. The missionaries invited Jack to perform the baptism. On December 31, 1968, Jack baptized the first thirteen Secoya Indians. What a glorious day!

Of course, most of our days in Ecuador were involved with the Russian radio work. Our hearts were focused on giving the good news of the Gospel to the entire Russian world. We prayed earnestly before each broadcast for God to touch hearts with the message about to be given. Jack spent many hours each week preparing and delivering sermons. Special programs were prepared for children, for women, and for youth. Other programs featured Bible lessons, as well as questions and answers from the Bible.

The Post Box program became very popular. Everywhere people listened, hoping to hear if we had received their own letters or not. I will never forget a letter from a dear lady in Russia. She wrote, "When I heard over my radio that you received my letter, I was so excited I did not know if I should run outside and shout the great news to my neighbors, or jump up and down in front of my radio receiver. I did the latter, shouting 'Praise the Lord, praise the Lord!'"

At Voice of the Andes we always dedicated a hymn to those whose letters we had received. How eagerly we had waited for those letters. We rejoiced over every letter that broke through barriers to reach us. Listeners shared their joys and sorrows, their stories, and their prayer requests. Many sent us photographs of their families, or small gifts, as well as postcard pictures of their home towns. There were those who even composed poetry. Here is one that sister Luba from Brazil dedicated for the fifteenth anniversary of the Russian ministry of Voice of the Andes.

[Original poem in Russian for 15th year of HCJB Russian radio programs in 1956]

The Fight of Faith

Fight, you loyal servants of God,
And labor for the glory of Christ.
Preach the way of salvation,
And call sinners to bow before Him!

Carry the words of the precious Gospel,
Over mountains, jungles, and oceans.
Go to the ends of the earth,
Wherever people are lost in their sins.

Keep working hard and long,
Awaken millions of people,
Arouse the sleeping Christians,
For our Lord is coming soon!

Your labor for God is not in vain.
Your reward is awaiting you in Heaven.
Keep working dear servants of the Lord,
And He will give you the needed strength.

Our days on earth will soon be gone,
Before God's judgment seat we'll stand,
Where you will see the results of your labor,
When the fruit of the Gospel is presented to Christ.

For fourteen years your work has gone forward.
The fifteenth one is ahead of you now.
Labor with courage and with your whole heart,
Go forward with the message of Christ!

But most wonderful of all were the letters from those who had come to Christ, those who had found new life in Him beside their radios. Many of them were remarkable stories.

Missionaries Stella Jarema, Elodia Kuvshinikov and Ruth Petrovna
collecting letters from the HCJB Post Office in Quito.

I recall one bright, sunny Quito day when we opened our mail box and found several letters from Russia and one letter from Poland. Opening the letter from Poland first, we found a long, long letter from Tamara in which she unfolded the story of her life. Let me tell you about her.

Tamara lived with her parents on a plot of land near a small town close to the Belarus border. There they grew cabbages, beets, onions, garlic, carrots, tomatoes, and lots of potatoes. When she was born and her father found out that he had a daughter, he became very angry. He wanted a son.

He needed a son, someone to help in the fields, to care for the animals, and to work in the garden.

As Tamara grew up and her parents had no other children, her father decided that she would be his boy. He made her work very hard. She recalled going out to the barn every morning to help feed the animals and to clean their stalls, of weeding in the garden, and of gathering the eggs. When she was a little older, her father sent her alone with the cattle to pasture. She would sit and watch so that they would not stray, and then she would bring them home again in the evening. No matter what the weather, whether sunshine or cold, Tamara had to fulfill her duties. Her father would not even allow her to wear a dress. No hair ribbons were permitted. She was to be the "boy" her father needed!

She was allowed to go to school only on rainy or very snowy days. Nevertheless, because she longed to learn to read and write, she would study on her own at home in the evenings. For this she was punished for being lazy. Many a night she went to bed crying. Her father did not allow her to have friends who would only "waste her time." Nor could she go to town or visit the neighbors. Her memories consisted of working in the field, digging, planting, and weeding. Always weeding!

She never knew what it would be like to sleep late into the day. Early every morning her father woke her gruffly and reminded her that "the field is waiting and there is much work to be done." She mentioned looking at her hands and feet. "They are so rough, with cracked skin or hard callouses," she wrote.

Her face was rough and red from constant exposure to the weather, and often it was very painful.

Her life was full of tears. She feared her parents and realized they did not love her. She was tired and lonely. She felt empty and restless. Her future looked dark. There was a time she considered ending her life, but even that thought frightened her, and she just shed more tears.

About that time, after a trip to town, her father brought home a short-wave radio. It was as if a friend had come to visit their home! Of course her father was the only one who was allowed to choose the programs. But Tamara welcomed this new addition into their lives.

One morning she awakened very, very early. It was still dark outside. Her parents were still asleep. She looked longingly at the radio. Very quietly she crept to it and turned it on. She had watched how her father kept turning the dial back and forth. Now she tried this on her own. Suddenly she was startled to hear beautiful music. She placed her ear against the radio receiver and realized the music was in the Russian language. She kept the sound as low as possible.

When the music ended a man began to speak. His voice was kind. In his speech he said there was a special person who LOVED mankind. His name was God. He LOVED all people on earth as individuals. His love was so great that He sent His Son, Jesus, to die on a cross to pay for the sins of each man and woman. This speech-maker explained that all we need to do to have eternal life is to repent of our sins and to trust Jesus as our Savior.

We were to tell Jesus that we were sorry for our sins and then invite Him into our hearts. He would then become our Savior, and He would love us and care for us. He died to redeem us from our sins. But the amazing thing was that three days later He arose from the grave and is alive today!

What a startling message this was for Tamara. To think there was someone who loved her! Someone who cared for her! She cried and cried. "But these were a different kind of tears," she wrote.

They were tears of joy. She was hearing a new message. It was a message of love and hope. She longed to learn more and to understand this message better.

So day after day she awakened very early and turned on the radio. Several months passed by. Then one dark, early morning at the invitation of the voice on the radio, she got down on her knees by the radio receiver and prayed just like the preacher on the radio suggested. There by the radio, she repented of her sins and asked Jesus to come into her heart. She wanted His love.

Immediately, she KNEW that He was with her. Such a joyful feeling came over her. It did not matter anymore when her father screamed or abused her. She was upheld by God's loving arms! He loved her! She felt His comfort! The Lord was by her side!

As her letter continued, she told us that she was now 24 years of age. Her living situation and her work in the fields had not changed. Life continued to be difficult. Her parents still made her work hard. They were older now, and demanded that she do more of the work.

But life for her was easier now. Her attitude changed because her heart was now at peace. God loved her! He calmed her spirit as she often prayed to her Heavenly Father. When her parents mistreated her, she simply prayed and asked God for grace and patience. Oh yes, there were still tears. But they were no longer bitter tears. They were comforting tears as she felt the Lord's presence and His love for her.

When she told her parents that she had accepted Christ into her heart, they became more angry and hateful than ever. However, she was able to find an evangelical church in a nearby village, where she was warmly welcomed by other brothers and sisters in the Lord. She loved to go there and hear the reading of God's Word. Her father would only allow her to visit the church when it was raining or snowing. In her letter she admitted that she often prayed and asked the Lord to send rain or snow on church days.

With all her heart she thanked us deeply for every Gospel radio program. Over and over again she thanked us for showing her the way to God. "Now," she said, "I have a Heavenly Father. He loves me, and He has filled my heart with peace and joy!"

You can imagine how touched we were as we read her letter. One longed to reach out and hug her. As we answered her letter, we gave her the reassuring verse found in Deuteronomy 31:8 that says: *The Lord is the one who goes ahead of you; He will be with you. He will not fail you or forsake you. Do not fear or be dismayed.* Praise God that we know He is watching over dear Tamara even today!

Tamara's letter was one of thousands that came to us across the years. How we loved our radio listeners! Over and over again we thanked the Lord for the blessed privilege that He had given us to preach His Word over the radio. We were sad when after almost 30 wonderful years, the time came for us to return to North America.

We returned to the United States, where we worked in the main office of the Slavic Gospel Association. Jack continued to prepare and to record programs that were used on radio station Voice of the Andes until he became ill and could no longer preach. I continued to be involved in answering letters from the former Soviet Union. We also sent out many packets of Russian Gospel literature to many parts of the world.

After we left Ecuador and came to live in America, I had the wonderful opportunity to help care for my aging parents. As my father began to lose his physical strength, it was my mother who faithfully read the Word of God out loud. They would then spend time together in prayer. On July 26, 1987, my father went to be with the Lord. He was 89 years of age.

After the death of my Papa, Mama found it very difficult to live alone. During that same time my husband Jack was also in failing health, so we could not take her into our home. Then the Lord brought to mind the Russian Evangelical Baptist Center in Ashford, Connecticut. This wonderful facility is under the direction of the Russian Ukrainian Evangelical Baptist Union. Arrangements were made; Mama, Jack, and I moved there in 1989. Mama was given a cozy room in the Center's Home for the Aged. Jack and I were able to live in a small apartment on the same grounds of that Center. How Mama loved the daily morning devotions, the afternoon prayer meetings, as well as inspiring Sunday services. Everything was in the Russian language. I loved my daily visits with my mama!

Immediately I was able to engage in Russian ministry. Brother Platon Chartslaa, who was the Slavic Gospel Association Russian-language editor for many years, was busy preparing new Russian books. I was able to help with bilingual correspondence and documents. Soon there was the added ministry of teaching Bible during the many weeks of the children's camp program that was held in Ashford every summer. Not long after the tragedy of Chernobyl, 23 children from Belarus were sent to our camp for rehabilitation. What an experience it was to teach the Word of God to children who had never before heard about Jesus. How they questioned me. Some challenged me. I loved them all.

One Sunday morning during camp it was decided to bring the Chernobyl children into the Home for the Aged so that they could join with the older residents in a real Russian Gospel service. Just as the pastor prayed the closing prayer, one of the fifteen year old girls burst into tears and ran out of the building.

I ran after her. "Ira, Irachka," I said, "what is the matter?"

By now she was crying so hard she was shaking. Through her sobs she said, "All my life I have been told there is no God. But that is all you people talked about for the past hour. It is very upsetting to me."

And her sobs continued. I simply hugged her and held her until she stopped crying. But God's Word is powerful, and by the end of the two weeks of their visit, a majority of the children had asked Jesus to come into their hearts.

Mama spent four peaceful years in this blessed facility. Finally, at age 88 her physical strength began to weaken. It was Sunday evening, February 14, 1993. I saw that Mama was much too weak to go to church. I quietly helped her get ready for bed. Just before she lay down, she took my hand and kissed it and thanked me. I prayed with her, kissed her, and went to the evening service. That night my Mama died quietly in her sleep just as had my Papa! With all my heart I thank the Lord for my wonderful, precious parents who taught me to love God!

The months that followed were very difficult for me. I had become accustomed to seeing Mama sitting in her favorite chair at the Home for the Aged waiting for me. Usually her lips would be quietly moving. I knew she was praying. The first thing she would ask me every morning was, "How is Jack?" knowing that he was not well.

No matter what my answer, she would smile and say, "I am praying!"

Those words would carry me through the day. But now her chair was empty. There were no more prayers. And Jack's health began to deteriorate. I turned to God's Word for help.

Four months after Mama died, Jack became critically ill. At times he was in a coma. Early Sunday morning, on June 13, 1993, I telephoned Pastor Philip Somers and asked him to pray for Jack. Pastor Somers prayed with me on the telephone and then said: "Ruth, when you go to visit Jack today, take your Bible with you. Read God's Word to him. You will be amazed to see his reaction."

As soon as I finished speaking with the pastor, I took my Bible and went to the hospital.

Jack was awake when I entered his room. I sat by his bedside and began to read Psalm 23. *Even though I walk through the valley of the shadow of death, I fear no evil, for You are with me; Your rod and Your staff, they comfort me. You prepare a table before me...Surely goodness and loving-kindness will follow me all the days of my life, And I will dwell in the house of the Lord forever.*

Suddenly he smiled. He tried to raise his head. He became very excited. He heard. He understood. And I could see by his eyes that his heart was responding to these verses!

After almost forty years of marriage, my dear husband, Jacob Ivanovich Shalanko, died that night. He went to his heavenly home! He was 68. In Revelation 14:13 we read, *"Write, 'Blessed are the dead who die in the Lord from now on!'" "Yes,"* says the Spirit, *"so that they may rest from their labors, for their deeds follow with them."*

Chapter 3

Journeys to the CIS

Upon receiving the phone call from the hospital telling me that my dear husband, Jack, had died, I knelt by my bedside. With tears, I called on the Lord. "Heavenly Father! I know my dear one is with you. I know that he is healed. He is rejoicing. He is singing and smiling, and he is no longer in pain."

"And now Lord, what do you want me to do? I thank you for the good health and strength that I still have. Even if I am a widow, I want to continue serving You!"

I felt God's arms around me during those days of grieving.

It is amazing how often widows and orphans are mentioned in the Bible. God does care for the widows and orphans! There have been many lonely times, but I can testify to the Lord's presence and His care. In my times of sorrow,

He has filled my heart with peace and with the assurance that He is by my side.

Rev. Grigori and Nadia Komendant

It was several weeks after my husband's death that I received a warm invitation from Kiev. Sister Nadia Danilovna Komendant, then the women's ministry leader of the churches in Ukraine, was calling me. "Ruth Petrovna, please come and join us for the women's fall conference which will be held in Alexandria."

My heart beat faster. God was answering my prayers for service. However, I had never dreamed that it would be in the former Soviet Union.

After praying about this, I quickly answered her. Yes! I would go. And so I went. And how those two weeks in Ukraine were filled with blessed meetings. Everywhere former radio listeners clustered around me. Everyone told me how much the radio programs had meant to them. They told me what deep comfort and spiritual encouragement they had received.

The highlight of the trip was the weekend women's conference. Many ladies came by train. Others walked. They gathered from eight different communities. Once there, sisters from each church contributed to the program. There was a cascade of musical numbers, beautiful poetry, and moving testimonies. Nadia Danilovna, her precious mother, Maria Grigorevna Andrikevich, and I each gave messages.

The early breakfast was a highlight of the conference in Alexandria, Ukraine.

The morning program had begun at 10:00 a.m. and was to stop at noon for lunch. Nadia tried to close the meeting at 1:00 p.m. So prevalent among us was God's Spirit, the ladies begged her not to stop. Finally, at 2:45 p.m., the cooks said, "Sisters, we must eat. The borscht is boiling over and over."

I must say that borscht was delicious.

What a wonderful conference that was! Our hearts were blessed as we wept and prayed together. We thanked God for the spiritual uplift which each one of us had received.

Flying back to North America, I read Romans 14:12 which says, *Each one of us will give an account of himself to God.* And as I contemplated the past two weeks of ministry in Ukraine, I knew that I had to respond to His call. There on that plane I promised the Lord that I would continue to serve Him wherever He might lead me.

A year later an invitation came from Rovno, Ukraine, to participate in special church-planting seminars for pastors and Christian workers. The men were to bring their wives. Several single women who were engaged in missionary work were also coming. They asked me to speak to the women on subjects of particular interest to them. I dropped on my knees and prayed, "Lord, thank you for another opportunity to serve you. Guide me. And help me to bring your Word in spirit and in truth."

Now it was August 1994. The Komendant family met me at the Kiev airport, purchased my ticket, and put me on the night train for Rovno. About 60 women attended the eight days of seminars. During one session we studied Proverbs 31:10-30. There we learned what the true characteristics of a Godly woman are, whether she might be a wife, a mother, or a single lady. A godly wife speaks kindly to her husband. She helps, honors, and loves him. A godly mother works and cares for her children. She loves them. She encourages them and provides for their daily needs.

A godly single lady is eager to serve others. She should show kindness and concern to those around her. Only then, will we be blessed with the words that say, . . . *but a woman who fears the Lord, she shall be praised* (verse 30). There were many sincere and touching prayers at the end of that service. Women dedicated themselves to become better examples in their homes and their communities.

Later, among the women who came to speak with me, there was one special lady who deeply touched my heart. Short of stature, with dark, shining eyes and short, dark, straight hair, she spoke to me in broken Russian. She told me that she was from Yakut, near the Lena River, in far north-eastern Siberia. She and her husband had traveled almost a week from their home in Yakutia to attend this conference in Rovno, Ukraine. They had traveled both by bus and by train, changing trains several times during their long, long journey.

Turning her head from side to side and looking intently into my eyes, she said in halting Russian: "My husband and me ...we tell Yakut people about God. We have...six children...live far...far...away...where very, very, cold. I not know before...must love husband. I not understand this. I...change now. I will ...love...husband. I will...teach...six children better. I...want...make family...more happy. Yes...thank you...for... good lesson. I did not know...before."

She shook my hand, bowed slightly, and slipped away silently.

I cannot forget that dear lady, and often I pray for her. Later I learned that the only book of the Old Testament that had been translated into the Yakut language was the book of Genesis. She had never had an opportunity to read or study those verses in Proverbs 31. This Old Testament teaching was completely new to her. Thank the Lord that the New Testament has been translated into the Yakut language.

My last night in Ukraine was spent in the home of the Komendants. That evening we chatted about all the new opportunities which were opening up for Christian service in the CIS. Abruptly Gregory Ivanovich Komendant, one of the leading Evangelical statesmen of Ukraine, said, "Ruth Petrovna, leave your work in America and come to minister to our women here in Ukraine, Russia, Belarus, and Moldova while the door is open. Come this winter!" Nadia Danilovna spoke up, also, and added, "Join us for our women's winter conference in March. Encourage our women about how we should live as Christian ladies in this new era."

My heart stood still. What an invitation. What a challenge. Was this the open door I had prayed for ever since Jack had gone to be with the Lord? Nor could I escape Nadia Danilovna's final words of farewell as she waved to me at the Kiev airport and called out: "Come back, come back Ruth Petrovna, come back!"

As the huge airplane took off from Kiev, I closed my eyes and thanked the Lord for those wonderful weeks of ministry in Ukraine. During the long hours of travel, over and over again I heard Nadia Danilovna's parting words to me: "Come back, Ruth Petrovna, come back!"

"Oh Lord," I prayed, "show me Your will for the next steps of my life!"

As the weeks went by, God did answer my prayer! He gave me sweet peace. My heart was full of anticipation and great joy. I felt assured that God wanted me to return to the land of my roots. I met with Brother Robert Provost, the President of the Slavic Gospel Association. I told him my heart's desire was to continue serving the Lord among my Slavic people. He encouraged me whole-heartedly to take up the challenge of women's ministry in the former Soviet Union. He also suggested that I find a lady to accompany me during my travels there.

"Oh Lord," I prayed again, "who can help me? Please send me someone."

Platon Chartschlaa and Ruth Deyneka in Ashford in 2013

Almost at once the Lord supplied that lady! Brother Platon Chartschlaa for many years had been the Slavic Gospel Association's faithful chief editor. He was the overseer of the Russian version of the Bible Knowledge Commentary, as well as the editor of many, many other books which the Slavic Gospel Association had printed. When he heard that I needed a traveling companion, he quickly recommended his niece, Svetlana. Born in Abkhazia, Svetlana was now living in the Moscow area. Platon Chartschlaa died on July 1, 2015.

What a blessing Svetlana proved to be! She arranged all our travel details. She was my congenial companion and faithful prayer partner for those three months. She took very good care of me! How I thank the Lord for her!

And so it was that Christmas day, January 7, 1995, found me in Moscow, Russia, standing on the platform of the Moscow Central Baptist Church. "Dear Lord," I prayed, "am I really here?"

Senior Pastor Pyotr Borisovich Konovalchik invited me to give greetings. Standing in front of that crowded audience, I knew that many of them had listened to our radio broadcasts from Voice of the Andes in Ecuador. In past years we had seen them only in our imagination. Now I was captivated by their nodding heads and smiling faces. And to think that my Papa had spoken from that very same pulpit many, many years earlier!

After that Christmas morning service I began a venture with Christ across Russia, Ukraine, Belarus, and Moldova. Indeed, I returned again and again over the next nineteen years! Many times there were women's meetings in tiny hamlets and small villages. On other occasions meetings were held in great cities: Moscow, Samara, Omsk, Kiev, Odessa, Minsk, Kobrin, and Chisinau. Over seventy places in all!

The meetings themselves varied greatly. There was sweet fellowship in many Houses of Prayer. In Ukraine I told the entire work force of a factory (which produced stage clothing and theatrical costumes) that God loves them.

Of course, most of my gatherings have been with the dear women. What a variety these gatherings have proven to be: from a cozy group of five unchurched ladies in Lvov drinking tea together, to a group of lively teen-age single women in Kobrin, and with many widows. I feel so very rich with the abundance of new friends that the Lord has given me.

A Personal Moving Experience

I was in Belarus! I found the village of Staramlynia where my Papa was born in 1898. And there stood my Babushka and my Dedushka Deyneka's yellow house!

I saw the white fence that surrounded the old Deyneka property. I saw the well where my Papa had drawn water for his family. I saw the dirt road where my Papa had played as a boy. I had found my roots!

Neighbors quickly gathered and began to tell stories about my Papa and his family. An elderly man living across the road remembered the day in 1914 when my Papa left the village. The neighbor then went back into his house and brought out old photographs of my Papa which were taken on his visit in 1925.

By now my blind cousin, Anastasia, and her husband, Peter, were living in the old Deyneka house. What an emotional moment it was to meet my cousin Anastasia for the first time in my life. Oh the tears of joy!

I had found the place "where it all began." There I stood with a heart thankful to the Lord. I just praised Him and thanked Him for giving me this unexpected blessing.

As I walked away from my Papa's house, I stopped and turned around and looked back. I thought to myself, "What if ...what if my Papa had never gone to America? What if...I had been born in this village, in that house and had never heard about the Lord? Where would I be today?"

Immediately the verse in Jeremiah 29:11 came to mind, *For I know the plans that I have for you, declares the Lord. Plans for welfare and not for calamity to give you a future and a hope.* All I could say was, "Thank You Lord for the way You have led my life! And thank You Lord for this glimpse of my Papa's house and boyhood life in this village."

A few months later, the Lord gave me another special blessing in Belarus. I was invited to speak in a small church in the town of Dragichin, where my Mama had often attended as a young lady. Quite a group of the older ladies came an hour early to meet me and to tell me their memories of my Mama.

Once again, I experienced great emotion. Here I sat among those dear Babushkas with their big smiles, each one telling me about my Mama's sweet and kind ways and beautiful soprano singing voice.

These were her friends. "As a young lady your Mama was shy," one said.

In a whisper, another lady told me that my Mama was the prettiest girl in the church. Sitting together in a circle, each one was eager to mention something about my Mama. They all remembered how she loved to pray! What a beautiful heritage the Lord has given me!

Indeed, in all my travels throughout the former Soviet Union, there was always the same wonderful welcome from my brothers and sisters in Christ. And what a joy it was to often meet dear radio listeners. There would be hugs and joyful exclamations of welcome. We are never strangers when we are one in Christ.

I used stories of women in the Bible for our lectures. I told them that the very same Lord, who helped those women so long ago, is also here to help each one of us today. As we read the Scriptures together verse by verse, we saw God's faithfulness. We saw how we, too, can lean on Christ in our present circumstances. At the close of each session there was always a wonderful time of prayer. Some repented. Others opened their hearts to the Lord and called out for help and strength in their daily lives. Others rededicated their lives to Him.

Often the person in charge would open up the service for questions from the audience. I must say, the ladies did not hesitate to speak up! There never seemed to be a lack of questions! What I found were women who were seeking to know God better, women who wanted a closer walk with Him.

I began to hear a repeated petition. "Sister Ruth Petrovna, we need books. We need books written by Russian women who will encourage us in our Christian walk."

There was a memorable encounter with such ladies at the close of a weekend of special women's meetings about 500 kilometers east of Moscow. There they stood with me; lovely, educated, brilliant women. "In this church we have heard about God and His love. We have accepted Him. We are reading the Bible. We are praying for our unsaved husbands and children. However, we all grew up in a communist environment. Some of us even belonged to the Communist Party. We are university graduates, but we have no religious background whatsoever.

"What we really need is a book to help us GROW SPIRITUALLY and to show us how to mature in the Lord! It was good to have you with us. But we will not remember everything we heard. If only we could have such a book, we would read it over and over."

I cannot forget that challenge.

Rather, as time rolls on, the challenge has grown within me. At the same time, God has also given me a deep fascination with the Tabernacle, which is described in the book of Exodus in the Old Testament. God gave the Tabernacle's design to Moses during the time he was leading the children of Israel out of Egypt, through the desert, and into the Promised Land.

Today, we see how the Tabernacle and its furnishings not only held deep meaning for the ancient Israelites, but how lessons from that ancient sanctuary can also help us to grow spiritually in our own lives. The Gate, the Brazen Altar, the Laver, the Table of His Presence, the Lampstand, the Altar of Incense, and the Ark of the Covenant: everything in the Tabernacle is an illustration of how we can mature spiritually in the Lord even today!

The author of the book of Hebrews in the New Testament also knew this. He used the Old Testament Tabernacle and its furnishings to illustrate the Gospel to those first-century Jews who were learning to trust Christ as their Lord and Savior. So, in that same spirit, in these pages let us explore the Tabernacle's symbolism for us today in the twenty-first century. And let us do it in the spirit of King David, himself, who said in Psalm 25:4-5: *Make me know Your ways, O Lord; Teach me Your paths. Lead me in Your truth and teach me, For You are the God of my salvation; For You I wait all the day.*

Chapter 4

The Brazen Alter   The Altar of Incense

The Gate   The Lampstand

The Tent of Meeting

The Laver

The Table of the Bread of the Presence

The Holy Of Holies

The Tabernacle

Let us now begin our study of God's great object lesson for His people. It is found in the book of Exodus in the Old Testament. Here we read how for centuries the children of Israel had been slaves in Egypt. In that country they were mistreated and had suffered greatly. God saw their oppression. He heard their cries and was moved by their tears. He had pity on His people because He loved them so. God chose Moses to be the champion who would help rescue His people from all their misery.

God's call to Moses came to him while he was pasturing his father-in-law's flock in the wilderness. There, God appeared to him in a fire, a blazing bush that did not burn up. Moses was startled when God called to him from the blazing bush, telling him that he was to lead the Israelites out of Egypt. Surprised, Moses said to God, *Who am I, that I should go to Pharaoh, and that I should bring the sons of Israel out of Egypt?* (Exodus 3:11).

God's answer to him was, *Certainly I will be with you, and this shall be the sign to you that it is I who have sent you: when you have brought the people out of Egypt, you shall worship God at this mountain* (Exodus 3:12).

Moses felt so inadequate. But with God's words of assurance, "I will be with you," Moses accepted this arduous task!

Exodus 6:28-14:31 tells us how God led His people out of their land of bondage. Fleeing from the Egyptian army, the Israelites arrived at the shore of the Red Sea. There God performed a great miracle. The waters opened, giving the Israelites a safe highway of escape, and then closed over their Egyptian enemies who were pursuing them.

The Lord continued to direct Moses and the Israelites as they journeyed through the desert towards the Promised Land. It is hard for us to imagine what a great multitude of people they were as they made their way through barren, thirsty lands, thousands and thousands of them.

When the Israelites finally arrived at Mount Sinai, several times God called Moses away from his people to join Him alone in a cloud on that mountain top. Each time that God did so, He gave Moses many instructions. How interesting it is that this mountain was the very same place where, earlier, Moses had heard God's call to rescue His people.

During one of those meetings on Mount Sinai, the Lord gave Moses some new instructions. In Exodus 25:8, God told him, *Let them construct a sanctuary for Me, that I may dwell among them.* God explained to Moses that He wanted to have a special place where He could dwell with the Israelites. He loved them deeply. He longed to be in their midst. This would be a place where the people could have fellowship with Him. Yes, God wanted Moses to construct a sanctuary!

This sanctuary was to be a portable structure, built by the children of Israel under the supervision of Moses. Over and over again it would need to be dismantled and carried with them on their long journey to the Promised Land.

Moses actually spent forty days and forty nights on Mount Sinai, listening to God and writing down all His instructions. We have that conversation recorded in Exodus 25-31.

As we read these seven chapters, it is absolutely amazing to see what precise instructions God gave Moses concerning the design and construction of the tabernacle. It was to have an enclosed outer court for the brazen altar and the laver. The tabernacle itself (also called the tent of meeting) was to have two sections. First, there was to be the Holy Place where the priests would carry out their daily duties. Then there was also to be the Holy of Holies, where only the high priest could enter, and that only once a year.

The Lord carefully explained how to build each piece of furniture in the tabernacle. He gave the exact dimensions for each piece, as well as instruction as to where it was to be placed. He told what materials should be selected, what colors must be on display, and how each item should be used. God required complete obedience. And Moses obeyed Him in every detail! (Exodus 25:9).

We find it so interesting that the Lord even designated the two men who were to be the overseers of the construction of the tabernacle and its furniture. Their names were Bezalel and Oholiab. In speaking about these men in Exodus 31:3, God assured Moses that they were very special craftsmen. His divine wisdom would guide their understanding, their knowledge, and their craftsmanship. The Lord also gave explicit instructions for the preparation of all the tools and instruments that were to be used in the sanctuary.

We also read that God said, *I will dwell among the sons of Israel and will be their God. They shall know that I am the Lord their God who brought them out of the land of Egypt, that I might dwell among them; I am the Lord their God* (Exodus 29:45-46).

Moses listened to the Lord very carefully. He gathered together all the instructions that God had given him. Now he was ready to go down the mountain to report to his people.

Suddenly, the Lord gave Moses some very sad news. *Go down at once, for your people, whom you brought up from the land of Egypt, have corrupted themselves.*

They have quickly turned aside from the way which I commanded them. They have made for themselves a molten calf, and have worshiped it and have sacrificed to it (Exodus 32:7-8).

Poor Moses hurried down from the mountain. When he came near the camp, he saw a golden calf that the people had made. There they were, dancing and worshipping their idol. What a sad picture. It was just as God had said. The Israelites had corrupted themselves! How soon God's people had forgotten all the amazing things that He had done for them. It is so true; sin will destroy us if we fail to follow the Lord.

In righteous horror, Moses totally destroyed the calf idol. He questioned his brother Aaron: how could such a sin have come about? He heard Aaron's foolish explanation with disdain. With great sadness in his heart, Moses then called out to all the people. *Whoever is for the Lord, come to me!* (Exodus 32:26).

It must have been quite a scene to see all the sons of Levi step forward confidently to gather around Moses. He then sent these Levites out to punish severely those who had been running wild in idolatrous worship. After this, once more, Moses reprimanded the people for their horrible sin. Then he returned to Mount Sinai to continue his dialogue with God.

Eventually, Moses came down again from Mount Sinai. This time the people were amazed to see his shining face, radiant because he had been speaking with God. As soon as he returned, Moses called all of the people together. He had something very important to tell them! God had asked him to say to the Israelites: *Let them construct a sanctuary for Me, that I may dwell among them!* (Exodus 25:8).

How amazing! God wanted to fellowship with His people! He wanted them to construct a sanctuary. It would be a very special place, a place where He could meet with them and dwell with them.

Moses proceeded to tell them what else God had said (Exodus 25:2). God was requesting that the sons of Israel would bring in all the materials that would be needed for the construction of the tabernacle. It was God's desire that each Israelite would feel moved in his heart to contribute something that would be necessary. The Lord was looking for willing people to furnish all of the items needed for the tabernacle.

While Moses was on the mountain, he had written down everything God had told him about the tabernacle. He had made lists of all of the many things which God said would be needed. Now, as Moses read the lists and named all the items, the people stood at attention, listening intently.

First of all, large quantities of gold, silver, and bronze were needed. Then specific colors of thread and fabric were necessary for all the curtains, for the hangings, and for the coverings that were to be made: blue, purple, and scarlet. What beautiful colors! The tabernacle priests would also need oil for lamps, specific spices for anointing, and fragrant incense. Details were also given as to what type of cloth and skins were to be brought in.

God then explained their precise purpose and where they would be placed. Instructions were even given concerning the woven garments for Aaron, who was the high priest, and for the garments of his sons, who would carry out their priestly duties. God also specified that acacia wood was to be used for furniture, as well as for poles. Goat's hair, badger skins, and ram skins would also be needed.

Gem stones crowned the list: onyx, ruby, topaz, emerald, turquoise, sapphire, diamond, jacinth, agate, amethyst, beryl, and jasper. They were to adorn the breastplate. Yes, all these were items that God told the Israelites to donate towards the erecting of the tent of meeting!

After hearing all of these instructions, the people left Moses and went back to their tents. The Israelites had much to think about (Exodus 28:17-20).

What happened next was very heartwarming. Just listen to this.

Scripture tells us, *Everyone whose heart stirred him and everyone whose spirit moved him came and brought the Lord's contribution for the work of the tent of meeting and for all its service and for the holy garments.*

Then all whose hearts moved them, both men and women, came and brought brooches and earrings and signet rings and bracelets, all articles of gold; so did every man who presented an offering of gold to the Lord.

Every man, who had in his possession blue and purple and scarlet material and fine linen and goats' hair and rams' skins dyed red and porpoise skins, brought them. Everyone who could make a contribution of silver and bronze brought the Lord's contribution; and every man who had in his possession acacia wood for any work of the service brought it.

All the skilled women spun with their hands, and brought what they had spun, in blue and purple and scarlet material and in fine linen.

All the women whose heart stirred with a skill spun the goats' hair.

The rulers brought the onyx stones and the stones for setting for the ephod and for the breast piece; and the spice and the oil for the light and for the anointing oil and for the fragrant incense (Exodus 35:21-28).

And just imagine, the people brought everything that was needed. Everything! And they did it willingly!

No doubt many of these items were from the gifts which the Egyptian women had given the Israelite women just before they left Egypt. We read in Exodus 12:35-36 that the Israelites: *had requested from the Egyptians articles of silver and articles of gold and clothing; and the Lord had given the people favor in the sight of the Egyptians, so that they let them have their request. Thus they plundered the Egyptians.*

How wonderful it is to read that the Israelites now gave these same things to Moses with a willing heart. I think it shows that they, too, were longing for a place where God would dwell among them. I am sure there was great excitement as, day after day, the Hebrews watched all the work that was going on. And every day during the construction process, the people kept bringing whatever they could and whatever was needed. In fact, they responded so heartily that there came a time when Moses actually had to tell them to stop. Sufficient materials had been brought in! No more were needed (Exodus 36:5-7).

For months, the sons of Israel gave themselves whole-heartedly to the construction of the tabernacle and its furnishings. The day finally came when everything was completed.

Moses examined all the work that had been done. Under God's guidance he made sure that everything was set in its correct place. Finally we read, *Thus Moses finished the work* (Exodus 40:33). What a time of rejoicing! Everything was just as the Lord had commanded. They had worked long and hard, and now all was completed! And so it was that the glory of the Lord filled the tabernacle; there God dwelt among His people!

So, now, what does the tabernacle mean for us today, thousands of years later? For us the tabernacle is a great illustration of God's plan for man's redemption. It was a lesson given in the Old Testament, but it has meaning for all time. Certainly we Slavic people, with our great cultural heritage, can appreciate the beauty and the truth embedded in the symbolism of the tabernacle!

In that symbolism we can see:

❯ Jesus as the door of salvation
(the Gate)

❯ Jesus' atoning sacrifice for our sins
(the Brazen Altar)

❯ God's holiness that requires us to be cleansed from all sin
(the Laver)

❯ Christ as the Bread of Life, and the importance of our having fellowship with Him
(the table of the Presence)

❯ Christ as the light of this world
(the Lampstand)

❯ The importance of prayer
(the Altar of Incense)

❯ Reverence for God
(the Veil)

❯ The presence of God in the believer
(the Ark of the Covenant in the Holy of Holies)

Actually, we will see that each piece of furniture in the tabernacle can be an illustration to help us grow spiritually!

Chapter 5

The Gate

The tabernacle was surrounded by a courtyard. Enclosing that courtyard was a boundary wall that separated the tabernacle from the rest of the camp. The boundary wall itself was made of fine white linen hangings that were stretched tightly from one pillar to another. There were a total of 60 pillars. These pillars were placed in such a way that 20 of them stood on each side along the length of the courtyard. Ten pillars stood at each end of the area. All these courtyard pillars were strengthened with silver bands and had hooks of silver on top and sockets of bronze at the bottom. These helped stabilize the hangings attached to the pillars. This solid boundary wall kept animals and intruders from entering the courtyard (Exodus 38:17-20).

However, the front section was very distinct. It had four central pillars that did not have white hangings. These four pillars supported very bright, beautifully colored hangings in purple, blue, and scarlet yarn of finely-twisted linen. These hangings were the gate! Their bright colors clearly marked the entrance into the courtyard. This made it easy for the repentant Israelites to find the gate when they brought animals for the daily sacrifices. It was also through this gate that the priests themselves had to enter the courtyard. Indeed, this was the only entrance into the courtyard of the tabernacle.

This gate is a wonderful symbol of what our Lord and Savior Jesus Christ truly is for us sinners on this earth. In John 10:9 Jesus said, *I am the door.* There is only one way to God. Only one door. I have heard people say, "Oh, there are lots of different ways to God. One can choose whichever way he wishes." But the Lord Himself said, *I am the way, and the truth, and the life; no one comes to the Father but through Me* (John 14:6). We must remember that JESUS IS THE DOOR to salvation and to everlasting life with God Himself.

There are some people who listen to a presentation of the Word of God. They appear to be deeply interested and to be ready to repent of their sins. They seem ready to ask the Lord to forgive them, to cleanse them, and to make them His children. They go right to the very door itself!

Then, they stop. They hesitate. They begin to make excuses. They remember their worldly pleasures. They do not want to give them up. Sadly they turn around and go back, sorrowful, and without Christ. They will not take that last step to go through the door of salvation. Oh, how very sad.

I am reminded of something that happened several years ago. After leaving radio station Voice of the Andes in Ecuador, we were working at the Slavic Gospel Association office in the United States. One of my responsibilities was to answer letters from Slavic-speaking people who were living in many areas of the world. We were receiving letters from the former Soviet Union with many, many requests for literature. What a joy it was to fill envelopes and small parcels with Gospel literature and to send them to those who had asked for them.

Peter Jr., Ruth, and Peter Deyneka Sr. in Quito Equador

One day my brother, Peter Petrovich Deyneka, had an interesting idea. He, too, had once spent a year ministering at radio station Voice of the Andes in Quito. Now he remembered the many requests for New Testaments and Bibles from our radio listeners. In those days we had sent them books, but rarely did we know if they had been received or not.

"Why don't we ask the missionaries in Quito to send us some of the addresses of the people who had requested a Bible or New Testament?" my brother asked? "Then let's send them another copy, just to be sure that they indeed have one." Soon we received quite a few addresses from Quito, and with joy we mailed out many copies of God's Word.

Before long we began to receive letters of appreciation from those who received the Scriptures. How well I remember the day that we received a long letter from a young man in Russia. He began by describing his early life as an only child. He recalled that his parents were strong Christians. They had often endured harassment for their faith, but persecution did not dim their love for the Lord.

However, deep sadness entered their home when his papa became ill and died. Now there were just the mother and the son, and they were often lonely. His mama found great comfort listening to our radio programs. She spent much time in prayer, but her son began to distance himself from his mama's Lord. Rather, he spent time with the wrong kind of friends.

Coming home late at night, he would find his mama kneeling by her bed, praying for him. He tried coming home at a later hour, but he would always find her waiting on her knees, praying for him. Then one day she, too, became ill and died. How sad he was. She had been a wonderful mother, and he had loved her dearly. His only relief was that he was now free from seeing her pray for him, only to be disappointed by his unbelief.

Time went by, and he continued in his wayward ways. One day, coming home from work, he found a package in his mail box addressed to his mother. It had come from America. "Who would be writing to his mama from America?" he thought. With great curiosity he ripped off the outer wrappings. There in his hands he saw that it was a BIBLE!

His letter to us said, "When I saw this was a Bible, I felt as though a brick had hit me on the head. I fell to my knees, grabbed the Bible in both hands, and began to weep like a child. Memories flooded over me. I saw my Godly parents on their knees, praying and fellowshipping with the Lord. Once again I saw my dearest mama on her knees praying for me, pleading that I would open my heart and ask Jesus to come in.

"I could resist no longer. I cried out to the Lord and repented of my sins. I asked Him to forgive me. I opened my heart's door and asked Him to come in and be my Savior."

At the end of his letter he described how he could not put the Bible down. He began to read and reread it. On the following Sunday he almost ran to the House of Prayer. With his mama's new Bible under his arm, he went forward before everyone to repent and to pray! He had found his way to eternal life through Jesus Who is the only door! And God had answered his parents' prayers!

Dear ones, how wonderful that Jesus stands on the other side of the door. He calls us. He waits for us. In Revelation 3:20 Jesus says, *Behold, I stand at the door and knock; if any one hears My voice and opens the door, I will come in to him, and will dine with him, and he with Me.* This is amazing. Jesus is standing outside the door of our heart and calls us to Himself. Not only does He call us, He knocks on the door, trying to get our attention. He is knocking because He wants to come into our hearts. He wants to give us salvation. Oh, how He loves us!

Jesus does not demand. He does not force us. He lovingly calls us and knocks on our heart's door.

He wants us to invite Him into our heart. He is the only Way. He is the only Gate. I trust that you, too, have entered through the gate and have given your heart to the Lord Jesus Christ. If not, may you do so, even today! Remember, He stands at your heart's door knocking! Knocking!

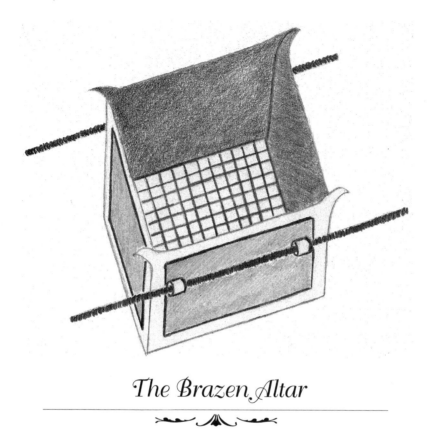

Chapter 6

The Brazen Altar

Just as the Lord gave Moses instructions as to how the tabernacle was to be built, so He also gave Moses instructions for all the functions that were to take place within the tabernacle area.

Inside the gate of the tabernacle courtyard was the great brazen altar. It was the very first thing that you would see when you entered the courtyard enclosure. This brazen altar was the largest of the seven pieces of furniture in the tabernacle. It stood on a mound of earth, rising higher than the other furnishings. It was the place of sacrifice and cleansing from sin.

The altar itself was actually made of acacia wood, a wood which came from a tree that grew well under the adverse conditions of the desert. Also, Moses made horns on its four corners; the horns were made of one piece with the altar. Since there was a fire burning on the altar day and night, the entire surface of the altar and the horns were protected by being overlaid with bronze. The grill of the altar was also made of bronze. The fire on the altar that consumed the sacrificed animals was never allowed to go out. (Exodus 38:1-4)

Every Israelite knew that it was only through an innocent animal being slain on his behalf that he could have a close relationship with Jehovah. So a person who had sinned was to bring a male animal with no defects to the priest at the gate of the tabernacle. In Leviticus 1:4-7 it says, *He shall lay his hand on the head of the burnt offering, that it may be accepted for him to make atonement on his behalf. He shall slay the young bull before the Lord; and Aaron's sons the priests shall offer up the blood and sprinkle the blood around on the altar that is at the doorway of the tent of meeting. He shall then skin the burnt offering and cut it into pieces. The sons of Aaron the priest shall put fire on the altar and arrange wood on the fire.*

This altar held great meaning for the children of Israel! It was the place where the priests offered the animals which the people brought as a sacrifice to God. We can picture in our minds all the confusion and the noise that was constantly going on near the gate of the courtyard as people arrived with their animals: a bull, a ram, a goat, a turtle dove, or a lamb. They were to offer their very best. There they would stand, waiting for the priests to come and take their animal as a sacrifice. These sacrifices were to atone for the people's sins and to maintain a right relationship with a Holy God. They were to be sacrificed on the brazen altar in the tabernacle courtyard!

There an Israelite would lay his hand upon the head of his offering, thus identifying himself with that sacrifice. The priest would then slaughter the animal, sprinkle some of its blood around the altar, burn the sacrifice, and pour the rest of the blood at the bottom of the altar. Every time an Israelite sinned and wanted God's forgiveness, he had to repeat this ritual.

As we look at the brazen altar, what does it mean for us today?

Now we can see that these animal sacrifices were only symbols of something much greater. Just think, the children of Israel had to repeat their symbolic offerings over and over, year after year. But today we can see that these offerings were all pointing toward that one great sacrifice that provides atonement for the sins of all people over all the ages, the sacrifice of God's only Son, the Lord Jesus Christ, on the cross of Calvary!

It means that we see Jesus, the Lamb of God, on the cross! What a powerful, vivid picture of God's greatest sacrifice, the ultimate sacrifice for our sin. What an act of love!

Walk with me through that great story. The night before Jesus was crucified on the cross, He spent an agonizing time of prayer in the Garden of the Mount of Olives. Luke 22:42-44 tells us how Jesus walked a short distance from the disciples who had accompanied Him there, knelt down and prayed. *Father, if you are willing, remove this cup from Me; yet not My will, but Yours be done.* Then we read further, *. . . being in agony He was praying very fervently; and His sweat became like drops of blood, falling down upon the ground.*

Suddenly the quietness of the garden was broken by the voices of rough soldiers, who came marching up noisily carrying swords and clubs. They grabbed Jesus, tied Him up, and took Him away.

And then the cruelty began. Soldiers bound Him and struck Him in the face. Later they whipped Him, hit Him with their fists, and spit on Him. In Matthew 27:28-29 we read that *They stripped Him, and put a scarlet robe on Him. And after twisting together a crown of thorns, they put it on His head, and a reed in His right hand; and they knelt down before Him and mocked Him, saying, "Hail, King of the Jews!"*

They tormented Him and humiliated Him. Then they took off the scarlet robe, put His own garment back on Him, and led Him away to be crucified. He had passed many hours without food or drink. His body was overwhelmed by weakness because of the cruel torture inflicted on Him.

After all of this, He was made to carry the heavy, wooden cross on which He would be crucified, to the place of crucifixion. He was taken to the place called Golgotha. There they nailed Him to the cross. Crucifixion was agony. What a cruel way to die! What pain and what immense suffering!

After He had agonized on the cross for hours, and with His strength ebbing away, those surrounding the cross heard Jesus' last words: *'It is finished!' And He bowed His head and gave up His Spirit* (John 19:30).

Jesus, the Son of God, willingly laid down His life on the cross as full payment for our sins. There are no further works of merit that we can possibly do in order to receive salvation. Christ has truly paid the full redemption price for our sins by dying on the cross and by shedding His precious blood. Our redemption is now complete! Jesus paid it all!

Now, we must share this good news of our redemption with those who do not know it!

How well I remember when my Papa and I were in Brussels, Belgium, in 1950. There was a large group of Russian refugees living in a refugee camp outside the city of Brussels. It was a thrill to attend a Gospel service among them. For many it was the first time they had ever heard the Gospel.

At the close of the meeting we stepped outside into the sunshine. I greeted 14-year-old Georgina, one of the teen-aged Russian girls who had come to the service with her parents. We began to walk together down the road.

Georgina looked up at me and in a quiet, hesitant voice said, "Before I heard your testimony today, I did not know that a young person could invite Christ into her heart. I thought only old people could repent!"

What a joy it was to tell her that Jesus had suffered and died on the cross for everyone, young and old. Suddenly Georgina stopped. She expressed a desire to accept the Lord into her heart. She began to pray.

We both shed tears as she repented of her sins and invited Jesus into her heart. After we both prayed, I remembered the verse in Luke 15:10 which says, *I tell you, there is joy in the presence of the angels of God over one sinner who repents.* There were hugs and much joy in that corner of Belgium on that warm Sunday afternoon.

The next afternoon my Papa and I walked to the central square in Brussels. Many people were milling about that lovely afternoon. Suddenly I saw a sad sight. A group of poorly-dressed people were slowly crawling on their knees, toiling up a flight of stone steps to a large Cathedral in the center of the square. A short distance behind them was an elderly grandmother who was also painfully struggling up those rugged stairs on her bruised, bloody knees. At each step she paused and mumbled the words, "Forgive me, forgive me, forgive me." She looked so weary and in great pain.

How sad that those dear people did not understand that salvation is a free gift whose price has already been paid by Jesus on the cross! We cannot earn our salvation by what we do, but we receive salvation only by faith in what Christ has done for us at Calvary.

In the New Testament we read that John the Baptist was standing on the banks of the Jordan River. Suddenly he saw Jesus walking towards him, and he said: *Behold the Lamb of God, who takes away the sin of the world.* Jesus was that ultimate, true sacrificial lamb. With His death on the cross, He put an end to all other kinds of sacrifices for sin. (John 1:29)

For the children of Israel, the brazen altar was a place of atonement where they had to keep bringing animals time after time to offer as a sacrifice for their sins. But for us today, instead of repeated sacrifices on a brazen altar, we look to the cross where Jesus by His death has once for all paid the price of our sins!

When someone realizes that he is a sinner, he must do more than be sorry for his sin. He must determine to turn his back on sin. That is repentance. He must come to Jesus on the cross. Yes, to the cross! With great confidence we read in Ephesians 1:7 *In Him we have redemption through His blood, the forgiveness of our trespasses, according to the riches of His grace.*

I am so grateful for my Gospel heritage. When my brother Peter, sister Lydia, and I were children, we always enjoyed hearing the stories that our Mama and Papa would tell us about their younger days. One of our favorites was about the day our Papa asked Jesus to come into his heart.

He had never heard the Gospel story until he was nineteen years old and was living in America. He had begun to attend services in both the Russian language and in English. It was all so new to him and so very hard to understand.

In his own words he gave this testimony: "I enjoyed the singing very much, but did not like the preaching because when the minister talked I thought he meant me, and it seemed as if he knew all about my life. I was very uncomfortable. The Holy Spirit began to speak to me and I saw that I was a lost sinner, and I realized my need for Christ who died for a sinful world, including me."

Some new friends invited Papa to attend a Sunday afternoon Young Men's Bible Class. Papa's heart was touched as he listened to the presentation of the Gospel. He knew he needed to repent, but he was frightened.

To give himself courage, Papa decided to invite a friend to go to church with him. The young man agreed. All through the service Papa's heart was under conviction. Finally, as the meeting was coming to the end, Paul Rader, the pastor, called people to repentance.

The Deyneka Family, 1940

Papa was very moved, but he was afraid. Finally he leaned over to his friend and asked him, "Don't you want to go forward and accept the Lord?"

He thought if his friend went, he would go with him. His friend looked at him, shook his head, and said, "No, I am not going." But Papa could not hold out any longer. Forgetting about his friend, he almost ran to the altar. He fell on his knees. He cried as he prayed and repented of his sins. Jesus had died on the cross for sinners, and Papa knew that he was a sinner without Christ. That night he asked the Lord to forgive him and to come into his heart. And Jesus did!

As soon as he got up from his knees, he felt as though he were in another world. He shook hands with everybody standing nearby. His heart was bursting with joy. He looked around for his friend, but he was gone. Papa hurried home to the boarding house where he was living.

He burst into the house. In the lounge the owner of the house was sitting and reading a newspaper. He looked up and saw Papa standing there with a big smile on his face.

"Peter," he said, "have you been drinking?" "No Sir, I am not drunk," he said. "Well, you look drunk to me," answered the man. "Oh, no. You see, I got saved tonight," Papa explained.

But the man shook his head and said, "Listen, Peter, you better go right to bed and sleep it off, or you will be fired from your job tomorrow for being drunk. You can tell me all about it in the morning."

The next morning Papa awakened early. He could hardly sleep. He was bursting with joy! He knew that he was a child of the Heavenly Father, and that his sins were forgiven. Suddenly his greatest desire in life was to tell everyone that Jesus had shed His blood on Calvary so that anyone in the world who trusted in Him could be saved from his sins.

My Papa had found the way to eternal life! He repented of his sins on January 18, 1920. He always celebrated that day with joy and thanksgiving to God!

How wonderful that we, too, can find eternal life, just as Papa did. First we must open the door of our hearts and invite Jesus to come in. In the days of the children of Israel there was only one entrance, one gate, through which they could enter the courtyard of the tabernacle.

Then came Calvary. Now we must come to the Cross of Christ. There He died for our sins. We all need to repent, ask Him to forgive us and cleanse us of our sins. *These things I have written to you who believe in the name of the Son of God, so that you may know that you have eternal life* (I John 5:13).

How well I remember the first Easter that Jack and I spent in Quito, Ecuador, in 1955. There we discovered that all the evangelical churches held special services from Palm Sunday until Easter Sunday. They referred to those days as Holy Week. Every night there were sermons explaining the great price that Jesus paid by His death on the cross in order to ransom us from our sins. Many non-churched people attended these services, as well as those who already knew the Lord.

What I remember most vividly was a special hymn those great Holy Week Hispanic congregations would sing over and over again: Bleeding Hands of Jesus! What a hymn! Each verse describes the pain, the agony, and the suffering that Jesus bore while dying on the cross for the entire world.

I cried. The words spoke to my heart. They reminded me of how Christ suffered, bled, and died for my sins and for the sins of all mankind. It wasn't long before Helen Zernov, a missionary of the Slavic Gospel Association who was also preparing programs for Voice of the Andes, translated this hymn and others from the Spanish language into the Russian language.

We sang it repeatedly on the radio. Listeners loved it and requested the words and music. You can imagine how thrilled I am to see it included in the present-day Russian hymnals throughout the former Soviet Union.

Hands of the Redeemer

Bleeding hands of Jesus, crucified for me;
Hands that suffered torment, pain and agony.
Pierced by my transgression there on Calvary.
By the blood I'm ransomed and from sin set free.

Out upon the desert thousands needed bread;
Jesus, with compassion said: "These must be fed."
Then those hands of mercy multiplied the loaves.
Food there was sufficient for the hungry droves.

Hands that healed the lepers, made the blind to see;
Blessed hands of Jesus, wounded on the tree,
Knock upon your heart's door, knock so patiently.
If you bid Him welcome, free from sin you'll be.

At the cross we have been forgiven! There the penalty of our sins was paid by the Lamb of God. There Jesus Christ completed His work of redemption. In fact God said, *And their sins and their lawless deeds I will remember no more* (Hebrews 10:17). Because Jesus Christ has finished His work of redemption, with complete faith we can put our trust in Him. With confidence we can make John 3:16 a very personal verse. We can say, *For God so loved the world that He gave His only begotten Son, that whoever...* [Ruth Erdel or place your own name]...*believes in Him should not perish, but have eternal life.* And so a new life begins in us the moment we receive Jesus into our hearts. We begin our journey with Jesus!

Chapter 7

The Laver

In the courtyard, just beyond the brazen altar, stood another piece of furniture. It was called the laver. It stood near the entrance to the Holy Place. The laver's function was to hold the water, which was needed for cleansing.

But first let us describe how it was constructed. Both the basin and its base were made from bronze. Much of this bronze came from highly polished brass mirrors which the Hebrew women freely gave for its construction. These mirrors, no doubt, had been given to them by their Egyptian neighbors as the Israelites were leaving Egypt. Now they were melted down to become part of this beautiful bronze basin (Exodus 30:18-19, 38:8).

What were the specific instructions concerning the laver? The Lord said, *Aaron and his sons shall wash their hands and their feet* [in the water] *from it* (Exodus 30:19). Yes, we see that each time they entered the tent of meeting, they had to thoroughly cleanse themselves before they began to perform their priestly duties in the Holy Place. The importance of this cleansing was stated very clearly in Exodus 30:20 where we read, *when they enter the tent of meeting, they shall wash with water, so that they will not die.*

There was a real, physical need for this cleansing. We must remember that the tabernacle was constructed in the desert. There was dust and dirt everywhere. Probably there were many dust storms. We are not sure if the priests wore sandals or just walked barefoot, but either way, their feet were always becoming dusty and dirty. I imagine sand or dirt got in between their toes. We also know that there was no pavement in the courtyard or in the tabernacle area. The priests' feet were in constant contact with the bare earth as they walked back and forth from one end of the courtyard to the other. They had to thoroughly cleanse themselves each time they entered the tent of meeting to fulfill their duties.

Moreover, all day long the priests were involved in assisting the Israelites who came to present their sacrifices. One such example is found in Exodus 29:10-12 where we read of them slaughtering a bull before the Lord as a sacrifice. A priest had to put some of the blood of the bull on the horns of the altar with his finger and pour out all the blood at the base of the altar. The priests' hands would become unclean and smeared with blood. We cannot even imagine the number of Israelites who would come daily to present their sacrifices. The priests' work was never done. This means that the priests had to be on their feet the entire time, busy serving in their priestly duties and constantly going to the laver for cleansing.

Since the Hebrew women had given their highly-polished brass mirrors towards the making of this laver, the priests would catch a vision of themselves in the polished surface of the vessel. Its mirror-like surface helped the priests to see any uncleanness that they had not already noticed on themselves. This constant reflection reminded them that they must be clean in order to revere and worship Jehovah in a righteous manner. Every time they approached His presence, they had to be clean.

We can see that the laver was a very important piece of furniture in the tabernacle courtyard area. It was filled daily with fresh, pure, clean water! It stood at the entrance of the tent of meeting, the very spot where Aaron and his descendants constantly passed by. No matter how many times a day the priests might enter the tent of meeting, each time they had to cleanse themselves. THE LAVER WAS TRULY A PLACE OF CLEANSING!

The Laver as a lesson for us today

Do you remember the joy that swept over you on the day you repented of your sins and asked the Lord Jesus Christ to wash them all away? I do! God became our Heavenly Father and we became His children. The peace that we experienced was something that we had never thought possible. We repented. God forgave us. We were been born again as spiritual babies, and we began a new life with Him!

Then came the day that we were baptized. On that day we gave a public testimony that Jesus had forgiven our sins. Now we were identifying with the crucified, buried, and risen Savior. Baptism signifies death to sin and a new life in Christ. As we were baptized, we rejoiced that the Holy Spirit now lives within us and that we desire to live a holy life. We did all that in obedience to Him.

But then something happened. We awakened one morning realizing that we were still far from being perfect. Some of our sinful habits still troubled us. At times, unkind thoughts still entered our minds. We said things that we should not have said as born-again Christians. We often felt defeated.

So where can we find the answers for our problems with temptation and sin? Where can we learn how to grow spiritually? We need help.

And there is help! Our answers are found in the Bible! Let me tell you about the Bible!

The Bible is no ordinary book. It is divinely inspired by the Holy Spirit. In II Timothy 3:16 we read, *All Scripture is inspired by God.* Moreover, it was written under the Holy Spirit's inspiration by more than 40 human authors from all walks of life. They were priests, tent-makers, shepherds, farmers, philosophers, kings, musicians, physicians, and fishermen! The entire Bible contains 66 books, found in two distinct sections.

The Bible is a masterpiece of literature. It is a collection of poems, songs, biographies, histories, letters, sermons and prophesies. Together, they show us God's love and concern for His people. The eternal God does not change and neither does His Word. In Christ's own words in Matthew 24:35 we read, *Heaven and earth will pass away, but My words will not pass away.* These are very reassuring words.

Originally written in Hebrew, Aramaic, and Greek, the Bible has been translated into more than 2,000 languages. In 1454 A.D. it became the first book ever to be printed in any language. Four centuries later, the Holy Synod of the Russian Orthodox Church made a decree to translate the Bible into the modern Russian language. With the ardent labor of many scholars, and after years of interruptions, the translation was finally completed and printed in 1876. It was referred to as "Синодальный" (The Synodal Bible).

The supply of Russian Bibles was always limited because the demand for them was very great. By 1924 it is said that the stock of Bibles was almost exhausted, and the door to import Russian Bibles had been closed.

Then in 1926 Ivan Stepanovich Prokhanoff of Leningrad miraculously obtained the necessary permits from the Russian government to do a large printing of the Russian

Bible. He went to the United States of America to try to raise funds for this printing.

While in New York City, Brother Prokhanoff met my father, Peter Naumovich Deyneka, at the end of 1926. Brother Prokhanoff invited my father to join him in his ministry and to help him. Following this, my father preached in many churches throughout America. There he earnestly presented the need for funds to print Russian Bibles. The Lord blessed, money was raised, and 35,000 copies of the Bible and 25,000 New Testaments were printed during 1926, 1927, and the first five months of 1928. However, after that Prokhanov was not allowed to print any more Bibles in Russia.

In his book, *In the Cauldron of Russia*, Ivan Stepanovich wrote that "He [God] did what was impossible for us to attain. This was a gift from God and the American Christians to the Russian people in the time of famine for the Word . . . *Not to us, O LORD, not to us, but to Your name give glory because of Your lovingkindness, because of Your truth* (Psalm 115:1). Ivan Stepanovich Prokhanoff died in Berlin, Germany, in 1935.

Now let us take this BIBLE into our hands and learn from its pages. Remember, it is our guide book. Just as the laver provided cleansing for the priests of ancient Israel, it will teach us how to live a clean and pure life. It will teach us how to grow spiritually. As we begin to read the Word of God, let us do so with faith, with humility, and with prayer!

We remember that the laver stood near the entrance into the tent of meeting. It contained pure water which the priests used to wash the filth from their hands and feet. We saw that Aaron and the priests could not render service in the Holy Place until they had first thoroughly cleansed themselves.

That cleansing by the priests is a symbol of what we need to do in order to live a clean and holy life. The Bible is the mirror that shows us when we need cleansing. As we read the Scriptures, we will see our sins and impurities. But a mirror can only reflect what is on the outside.

However, God's Word is also like an x-ray. It shows us what we are really like on the inside and points out the areas in which we need to be cleansed. It is only when we are in the presence of the Lord that He will show us our flaws and sins. That is why it is so important to read the Bible daily. As we read His Word, it shows us our hidden impurities. As we pray and ask Him to forgive us, and cleanse us, we will once again have His peace in our hearts.

Many times while reading His Word we find help for the specific problems that we are facing, and this encourages us. How many times the Bible guides us, counsels us, teaches us, and inspires us! Happiness comes from the Word of God. The more we read the Bible, the more we will discover the hope and comfort that comes through God's mercy, grace, and forgiveness in Christ!

On the other hand, there are those times when the Bible shows us the wrongs we are doing. Wrongs, perhaps, that we do not even recognize ourselves. Or we may call them nothing more than bad habits, or little mistakes. Or we may try to excuse ourselves by saying, "This is my nature. I cannot help it."

Colossians 3:8 says we cannot excuse ourselves, *But now you also, put them all aside: anger, wrath, malice, slander, and abusive speech from your mouth.* Here again, God's Word is like the mirror surface of the laver. It shows us where our behavior is actually a sin. Any anger, malice, gossip, slander, or abusive speech towards someone is not pleasing to God.

Or perhaps there was an occasion when we were talking with friends. As our story proceeded, it was so easy to add something that was not true. We enlarged our story. Actually, we lied. Perhaps we tried to make ourselves look better. "Such a small thing," we say. "Oh, just a little lie."

But in Colossians 3:9 we read, *Do not lie to one another, since you laid aside the old self with its evil practices.*

God's Word shows us that it is very wrong to lie. It is never right to lie, for lying is an "evil practice." In Ephesians 4:25 we read, *Therefore, laying aside falsehood, speak truth each one to you with his neighbor, for we are members of one another.*

We must stop lying. We must ask the Lord to forgive us and to cleanse us. It is like going to the laver for cleansing so that we can stand clean and pure before our Holy God.

God's Word often convicts us. It corrects us and shows us how to live pleasing in His sight. Recently I read a story about a young evangelist. He was invited to preach in the House of Culture in a neighboring town. Large posters with his photograph were hung at many bus stops around town. They were advertising his special evening Gospel meetings.

On the first day of these meetings, one of the city buses stopped to pick up passengers. Among them was the evangelist. The bus driver recognized him immediately from all the advertising photographs he had seen around town. After the man stepped into the bus, he handed this bus driver a large bill to pay for his passage. In a very professional manner, the bus driver gave him his ticket, and a handful of change. The preacher sat down in the back of the bus and counted his money before placing it into his pocket. He noticed that there was an excess of two kopecks. He counted his change again and realized the bus driver had mistakenly given him too much money.

Well, what were two kopecks? Nothing, really! But in that moment the evangelist also knew that keeping it would be the same as stealing. And didn't the Bible say, *You shall not steal?* (Exodus 20:15). Of course, he would return it.

In the meantime, the bus driver was intently watching the preacher's reaction via his mirror. Would he return the extra money he was given? When it was time for the preacher to get off, he went to the front of the bus and handed the bus driver two kopecks. "You gave me too much change, Sir."

The bus driver looked him straight in the eye. "I know I did! I did it deliberately! When you got on this bus, I recognized your face from all the photographs around town. I wondered if you were a really sincere religious man, or just a fake? I wondered if you would keep it. I now see that you are an honest, religious man. I want you to know, that tonight, I will be attending your Gospel service at the Cultural Center."

As we make our choices and our decisions in life, we need to constantly ask ourselves: what does the Bible say about this circumstance? When we turn to Him with clean hearts, He will guide us through every situation. In James 4:8 we read, *Draw near to God, and He will draw near to you. Cleanse your hands, you sinners; and purify your hearts, you double-minded.*

It is like going to the laver. Just as the priests had to wash their hands and their feet often, so we need to read God's Word daily and then ask Him to cleanse us. Only then can we have sweet communion with our Lord.

How well I remember one particular day in my childhood. I was sitting on the floor at the doorway of our little kitchen. My Mama was on her knees scrubbing the kitchen floor. As she worked, she often told me stories about Jesus. That memorable day she began describing a time when Jesus saw a group of people who had followed Him into the country side. There were so many people that Jesus climbed a hill, sat down in front of them, and began to teach. Then my Mama quoted one of the teachings that Jesus had given that day. It was Matthew 5:8: *Blessed are the pure in heart, for they shall see God.*

"My dearest daughter, I think this would be a good verse for you to memorize," she said.

Together Mama and I repeated it over and over again until I had memorized it well. "*Blessed are the pure in heart, for they shall see God. Blessed are the pure in heart, for they shall see God.*"

"Oh my dear little girl," she continued, "it is so important to have a clean heart! You want to see Jesus someday, don't you?" she asked.

Of course I did, and with Mama's encouragement, I repeated the verse again and again.

I have never forgotten that verse. In fact, it often rebukes me even today when I fail the Lord and do something that might displease Him. Often I have stopped and asked God to forgive me. Just as if I were standing at the laver, I ask Him to cleanse me. I want to have a clean heart.

By being cleansed we restore our fellowship with Him. What a sweet peace comes upon us after we have prayed and asked the Lord to forgive us and to cleanse us. He takes us by the hand, and we hear His loving words: *For I am the Lord your God, who upholds your right hand. Who says to you, 'Do not fear, I will help you.'* (Isaiah 41:13). How wonderful that He holds us by our right hand and promises to help us. Then, why do we fear?

The Psalmist David asked a question in Psalm 24:3. *Who may ascend into the hill of the Lord? And who may stand in His holy place?* Then in verse 4, David himself gives the answer. *He who has clean hands, and a pure heart, Who has not lifted up his soul to falsehood.*

There it is again: clean hands, and a pure heart. Just as the priests had to cleanse themselves repeatedly at the laver, we too need to come to the Lord repeatedly for cleansing. When there is something in our lives that is not spiritually clean, we ourselves realize that our fellowship with the Lord is broken. If we sin, it is impossible to grow spiritually until we ask God to cleanse us. Only when we are cleansed will we be able to perceive the deeper things of Christ.

What about the temptations that come our way? And they do come. Praise the Lord, we can find strength to overcome them as we faithfully read God's Word, and as we pray for strength to grow closer to Him.

We have the wonderful example of what Jesus did when the devil tried to tempt Him. Jesus kept quoting Scripture!

Matthew 4:1-11 tells us that Jesus was led by the Holy Spirit into the wilderness to be tempted by the devil. In verses 8 through 11 we read, *Again, the devil took Him to a very high mountain and showed Him all the kingdoms of the world and their glory; and he said to Him, "All these things I will give You, if You fall down and worship me." Then Jesus said to him, "Go, Satan! For it is written, 'YOU SHALL WORSHIP THE LORD YOUR GOD, AND SERVE HIM ONLY.'" Then the devil left Him; and behold, angels came and began to minister to Him.*

Notice that Jesus was actually led into the wilderness by the Holy Spirit Himself to be tempted by the devil. Temptation itself is not sin. Rather, sin is yielding to temptation. Jesus proved to us that He is indeed the Son of God because He was able to meet temptation without yielding to it and because He was able to overcome the devil. Jesus did so by quoting Scripture.

We should not be surprised when the devil tempts us. We have seen how he tried to tempt Jesus. The devil will also try to offer us things that will take away our love for our Savior. He may try to make us proud or dishonest. He may try to undermine our faith in the Bible. But we must be strong in His Word. As we face temptations, we can overcome them by the power of the Word.

Yes, even Jesus was tempted. But He was victorious! And by His power in us, we, too, can be victorious over sin and temptation!

For the ancient Hebrews the laver was placed in the courtyard of the tabernacle. It was there for the priests to cleanse themselves before entering into God's presence. Now, for us today, it is His Word that teaches us how to live a holy life. Let us read it with faith. Let us heed His teaching! Let us ask Him to cleanse us!

Chapter 8

The Table of the Bread of the Presence

Beyond the laver stood the tent of meeting. Its exterior was a multi-layered covering made of goats' hair, of rams' skins dyed red, and of porpoises' skins. God had declared this tent would be the place where He would dwell with His people. So, let us look within it with reverence (Exodus 26:7, 14).

Within the tent of meeting we see two sections: the Holy Place and the Holy of Holies. At the entrance of the tent of meeting there were five pillars of acacia wood, each overlaid with gold (Exodus 26:36). Hung from these pillars were long, flowing, blue, purple, and scarlet curtains of linen cloth, with embroidered patterns woven into their fabric.

These curtains provided easy access into the Holy Place. It was through them that the priests entered into the Holy Place by day or by night in order to fulfill their many duties.

Moses' brother, Aaron, had been chosen by God to be the first High Priest. This position was not something anyone could choose for himself. Only Aaron and his descendants, who were from the tribe of Levi, could be priests. Theirs was a high honor and carried great responsibility! They were to be holy and to live clean, undefiled lives (Leviticus 8:8-11).

These priests were also required to wear very special clothing while ministering in the Holy Place. Their garments were to be made of finely-woven cloth. Golden threads, skillfully cut from hammered gold sheets, were to be carefully woven into the blue, purple and scarlet fabric used for their robes. On the hems of the robes were bells of pure gold. These bells were interspersed between pomegranates of blue, purple, and scarlet material and twisted linen. Their tunics also were made of finely woven linen, as were their turbans and caps. Every single piece of clothing is listed in Exodus 39:1-31. All of these garments were to be prepared by skillful hands.

God had appointed Aaron and his sons to perform a great variety of priestly duties. First of all, they were required to set up their family tents encircling the tabernacle in order to protect it (Numbers 1:50-54). Another of their very important duties was to keep a fire burning on the altar day and night (Leviticus 6:13). Indeed, Aaron and his male descendants were the only ones who could offer sacrifices for the sins of the people.

We remember how these priests were required to wash their hands and their feet at the laver each time they entered the Holy Place. They needed to be thoroughly cleansed before they entered into the presence of the Lord. These priests were also the only ones who could enter the Holy Place. Even Moses himself was not allowed to enter it (Exodus 40:35).

Upon lifting the hangings that closed off the Holy Place from the courtyard, the priests were greeted on their left by the light of the golden lampstand. Since there were no windows to let in sun light, the light from the lampstand was extremely important.

In the center of the Holy Place, at the entrance to the Holy of Holies, stood the altar of incense. And on the right stood the table of the bread of the Presence.

The table that held the bread of the Presence was made of acacia wood overlaid with gold. All the utensils laid out on the table were also made of pure gold (Exodus 25:23-30). Most importantly, every Sabbath twelve freshly-baked loaves of bread were placed on this table.

Very fine wheat flour was used in making these bread loaves. Scripture tells us the exact amount of flour which was required for each loaf of bread. Great care was taken that the bread was baked just as God had commanded. Once baked, the twelve loaves of bread were placed in two rows of six loaves each.

Pure frankincense was also placed on the table of the bread of the Presence as a memorial to the Lord (Leviticus 24:5-7). There was a golden rim around the edge of the table, which we presume protected the twelve loaves from falling off. In Exodus 25:30 the Lord tells Moses, *You shall set the bread of the Presence on the table before Me at all times.* God is reminding His people that He loves them and that He is always with them. He wanted to dwell among them.

God gave Moses further instructions concerning the twelve loaves of bread. He told Moses that every Sabbath day fresh-baked loaves of bread were to be placed on the table. During the week Aaron and the ministering priests, invited by God, gathered around this table to eat these loaves of bread. There they stood feasting together! They ate the bread and experienced God's wonderful presence.

What a blessed time it must have been for them! (Leviticus 24:8-9). This was also the time when they, as priests, had fellowship with one another. They had been kept busy from morning until night, fulfilling all that was expected of them. As they stood by the table eating the bread of the Presence, they could pause from all their priestly activities and be refreshed by fellowship with the Lord and with each other. As the priests ate the bread together, they were nourished both physically and spiritually.

But the table with the bread of the Presence also reminded the entire nation of Israel that God desired their fellowship. He loved them! Over and over again He had reassured them that He would provide them food and protect them during their long journey. He would take care of them.

So the twelve loaves of bread that were placed in two rows on the pure gold table were given to remind the people of Israel of their constant need to depend on Him (Leviticus 24:6).

Indeed, God had shown His people His power over and over. He had provided them with manna and water. He had protected them from their enemies. And how could they forget the terrible plagues that the Lord had sent for their sake upon Egypt while they were slaves in that country, plagues that won their freedom!

Remembering all this, the Israelites were to seek God, to obey Him, and to desire His continuing presence. And because God loved Israel, God gave His people an everlasting covenant!

Now we might ask, "What is a covenant?" A covenant is a solemn promise. It could also be called a pledge or a vow. And here was God in His great love making an everlasting covenant with His people. The twelve loaves of bread that rested on the golden table were given to God's people as a sign of that eternal covenant between Him and the Hebrew nation. That covenant was God's promise that He would be with His people and that He would take care of them!

What a glorious promise! Sadly, God's people might forget that covenant or break that covenant. But God promised them: *it is an everlasting covenant for the sons of Israel* (Leviticus 24:8). God would never forget it!

So, what does the Bread of the Presence signify for us today? What does it teach us?

As we read of Aaron and his sons eating the bread of the Presence in the Holy Place, we see a deep spiritual application for each of us. We see that the bread that was placed on that table is a picture of the Lord Jesus Christ who said, *I am the bread of life* (John 6:48), and *I am the living bread* (John 6:51).

Let us think about what this means to us. Bread! The physical bread we enjoy at our table is one of the world's great foods. The very nature of bread is to provide energy and physical sustenance. We Slavic people know how important bread is. When we have bread on our table, we know it will satisfy our pangs of hunger.

I remember as a little girl how excited my brother and sister and I would be when Mama would place a freshly-baked loaf of bread on the table. For us there could be no better food. We stayed around that table until she cut three pieces, spread homemade grape jam on top, and gave each of us a slice. However, as delicious as that bread tasted, in a few hours we were hungry again. It was merely physical bread.

The Bible tells us of spiritual bread. Jesus said, "I am the bread of life."

There are three Scriptures where Jesus tells us that He is the bread of life! In John 6:35 we read, *I am the bread of life; he who comes to Me will not hunger, and he who believes in Me will never thirst.* In verse 48 Jesus again says, *I am the bread of life.* Then in verse 51 He said, *I am the living bread that came down out of heaven; if anyone eats of this bread, he will live forever; and the bread also which I will give for the life of the world is My flesh.*

How did Jesus show us that He was indeed the bread of life? Let us follow His story in the Gospels.

Jesus' first ministry was to call people to repentance. Soon He invited twelve men to join Him. These men became His companions and helpers. He began to teach them spiritual truths. Walking through the countryside with them, Jesus entered synagogues and began teaching and proclaiming the Gospel of the kingdom that was to come. He healed every kind of disease and sickness, even giving sight to the blind (Matthew 4:23-25). He blessed the children, and He helped the widows. At times, eager crowds gathered on a hillside or along a lakeshore. There He taught them that God's Kingdom was near. If they repented and believed the Gospel, they would enter that Kingdom.

On one such occasion, Jesus attracted a very large crowd. He felt deep compassion for them because they were like sheep without a shepherd. For long hours He had taught them many things (Mark 6:34-45). It had grown late, and they were hungry. The disciples wanted to send all the people away to their homes. But Jesus knew that they first needed to be fed. The Scriptures tell us that Jesus took five loaves of bread and two fish in His hands. He looked up toward heaven, blessed the food, broke the loaves, and divided the two fish. In that miraculous hour, there was enough food to feed five thousand men (John 6:1-11).

Jesus and His disciples then crossed over to the other side of the Sea of Galilee. It was not long before people began to look for Jesus once more. They found Him in Capernaum. "Rabbi, when did you get here?" they asked Him. Jesus immediately knew why they were looking for Him. It was because He had fed them and had satisfied their hunger. They had benefited from the miracle of the physical bread. But, they had failed to believe in Him as their Messiah.

It was then that Jesus said to them, *For the bread of God is that which comes down out of heaven, and gives life to the world. . . I am the bread of life; he who comes to Me will not hunger, and he who believes in Me will never thirst* (John 6:33, 35). Sadly, the people were still focused on the physical bread which He had given them. But the satisfaction that it gave was only temporary.

Rather, Jesus longed for them to know that He could satisfy their spiritual hunger. He invited them to believe in Him and to follow Him. If only they would believe in Him, their hearts would find deep satisfaction. They would no longer be hungry or thirsty in their souls.

Likewise, in the tent of meeting, the gold table with the bread of the Presence reminded the Israelites that God was with them at all times. He fellowshipped with them and loved them. He alone could satisfy them spiritually.

Feeding on His Word Today

In the New Testament Jesus tells us that He is the bread of life (John 6:48), and that He is the living bread (John 6:51).

We who live in the New Testament era and who are true children of God receive our spiritual nourishment from His Word. As we read the Bible, we can find the answers to our questions about how to grow spiritually! The food that sustains the believer is the Bible. Just as our bodies need physical food to survive, likewise our souls need the spiritual food that we find in the Word of God.

There are many different ways to study God's Word. One such way is to begin reading Genesis 1:1 and read on through the entire Bible. During the thirty years my husband Jack and I lived in Ecuador, it was his custom to awaken at five o'clock every morning to read the Bible and pray. During his lifetime, he read the Bible through 34 times before he became ill and could no longer do so.

I have read the testimony of the Evangelist Billy Graham who has preached in many countries around the world. Each day he reads the chapter of Proverbs assigned for that day according to the calendar. He also reads one Psalm each day, then a portion from the Old Testament, and finally a portion of the New Testament.

There are also special devotional books which have a series of daily Scripture portions along with a comment or thought on the theme of each day's Bible verses. Some believers use these devotional books together with their daily Bible reading. In whatever way we may read the Bible, as we meditate on the verses which we have read, these verses will stay with us throughout the day. They will encourage our hearts. In Psalm 1:2 the Psalmist wrote of the godly man, *But his delight is in the law of the Lord, And in his law he meditates day and night.* It is good to start the day with the Lord.

Recently I was invited to fellowship with a group of ladies in a large church near the Pacific Ocean. There I met Oksana, a lovely young mother. She told me that she had recently started a new plan in the way she was reading her Bible. She had begun with the book of Genesis and was now reading the Bible for about an hour every day. She hopes to have the entire Bible read in about three or four months. She has encouraged her children to do the same thing.

This sounded like such a wonderful plan. So I, too, have started reading through the Bible from the book of Genesis to Revelation. I also have an exercise book beside me. Whenever I read an interesting fact, I am writing it down in my exercise book.

Here is one such example that I wrote down. In Genesis 5:21-24 we read about Enoch who lived to be 365 years old. And the Bible tells us that during those years Enoch walked with God! What a wonderful testimony! How I am challenged to walk with the Lord day after day.

How good it is to end the day with His Word! It helps to clear our minds of all that went on during the day and to find rest in Him. Many days we have had painful experiences. Our hearts are heavy. How good it is to open the Scriptures and to hear God's voice of comfort.

This actually happened to me recently. I received some disturbing news concerning my loved ones. My heart was sad and heavy. Just before going to bed, I opened God's Word. The first verse I read was, *Cast your burden upon the Lord and He will sustain you; He will never allow the righteous to be shaken* (Psalm 55:22). I was so touched that I wanted to cry.

Then I read another portion of Scripture from the New Testament. *Why are you afraid, you men of little faith?* (Matthew 8:26). By now, I admit, I did cry. But those were tears of thanksgiving which fell, while in prayer, by faith, I took my dear ones to the Lord. God's Word gave me peace and encouragement. I was able to close my eyes and find rest in Him.

I also heard of a lady who reads through one book of the Bible at a time. This is how she does it. She opens her Bible to the book that she has selected. She reads a few verses in the morning, places a marker at that stop, and leaves her Bible open. She has responsibilities that she needs to attend to and may be gone for several hours. Upon returning home, she sits down and takes her Bible and continues to read from where she had stopped reading earlier in the day. Again she marks that place, leaves her Bible open, and goes on to her next responsibility. All day long she keeps her Bible open and her place marked, and she returns to read it throughout the entire day.

After Jack's sister Neela retired, she had more time in the mornings to read her Bible. She prepared a small area in her tiny apartment where she put her Bible, a Bible concordance, a notebook, and her pen. She would begin reading. When she came to a verse or passage that she did not fully understand, she would stop, look it up in her study books, and pray about it. Then she would write out her thoughts and continue reading and praying. She faithfully read her Bible until almost her last day on earth, when she died of cancer at the age of 82.

Let me tell you how God's Word has blessed my family over three generations. I have wonderful childhood memories of daily Bible reading with my Mama and Papa. When Papa was home, we would all sit around the table, and he would read the Bible to us. When he was not at home, but preaching in some faraway church, we three children loved to sit on Mama and Papa's bed for our Bible reading time. After reading the Bible, Mama would also tell us a Bible story. How we loved those stories! Then we would discuss them and try to imagine all the events that took place. Finally, we would kneel together and pray.

If my brother or I had been disobedient in any way during that day, this was the time that my parents would talk to us about it. They would try to teach us the importance of being obedient. My sister Lydia was the youngest, and I must say that I do not recall that she was ever disobedient. She was a very quiet, sweet little girl who was content to sit in a corner and play by herself.

However, my brother Peter and I often tested our parents' patience. At such times, my parents taught us to ask God for forgiveness. Those were good training experiences in our growing up years, and I thank the Lord for my upbringing. But along with their discipline, my parents always let us know that they loved us, and that God loved us, also.

I suppose this was why, as young parents, my husband Jack and I also established a daily practice of reading Scripture with our own children. Our son John (Vanya) and daughter Lydia (Lida) were born in Latin America. They received all of their elementary and high school education during the years we lived in Quito, Ecuador, as missionaries with radio station Voice of the Andes. In the morning, after breakfast, Jack would always read a portion of Scripture, as well as read a short story or a lesson on Christian living. After that Vanya and Lida took turns choosing a hymn or chorus that we would sing as a family. Then each one of us would pray. We started the day with our Lord.

The Shalanko Family, 1956

It was during this time of family devotions that we prayed for one another. I especially remember our prayers on those days when our children were facing difficult exams at school. I remember how we would often share a special letter from a radio listener who had sent us a prayer request. How many times we prayed for our missionary friends who were ill or had special needs! And then, best of all, I remember the joy of answered prayers! Those were good times, times filled with encouraging lessons for all of us.

God has blessed my daughter Lydia with two daughters, Gemma and Gracia. My son John has one daughter, Katrina. So I have three beautiful granddaughters. Both families live quite a distance from me, and I do not have an opportunity to see them very often. However, recently my son John and his lovely wife Maria came for a visit. I told John and Maria that I was writing a book for Russian-speaking women. I also mentioned that I was going to include an account of how as a family we had a time each day for reading God's Word together when we lived in Ecuador.

My daughter-in-law Maria immediately said, "Well, Mom, John and Katrina read the Bible, have a short lesson, and pray together every morning before she goes to her classes. Since I have to leave for work very early, my time to pray with Katrina is at night before she goes to bed."

You can imagine how happy I was to hear that. I thank the Lord that my granddaughter Katrina is learning to call on the Lord for help in her young life. Yes, it is very important for us to read the Bible with our family. Children grow up so quickly and are soon gone from the home. It is imperative for each family to find its own appropriate time for daily family devotions.

Throughout the Scriptures, we also see how important it is for us to fill our hearts with God's Word in order to be nourished spiritually. In Ezekiel 3:10 God said to the prophet, *Son of man, take into your heart all My words which I will speak to you and listen closely.* How can we know what He has for us unless we read His Word? We need to receive a fresh portion of His Word each day so that we can constantly hear His voice and draw closer to Him. The more we read the Bible, the more we will discover the hope and comfort that comes through God's mercy, grace, and forgiveness in Christ.

In life we face many decisions. Perhaps you have reached a time in your life when you are asking: "What should I do now?"

Open your Bible. Do you know what the psalmist wrote in Psalm 119:105? *Your word is a lamp to my feet and a light to my path.*

So, keep on reading God's Word. Keep on praying. The light of His Word will show you which path to take. *Make me know Your ways, O LORD; Teach me Your paths. Lead me in Your truth and teach me, for You are the God of my salvation* (Psalm 25:4-5). Always GOD will guide us as we read His Word.

My Babushka, Anna Demidovich, had never learned to read as a young girl. She spent her youth working in the fields in western Belarus and helping her family in their household chores. When she accepted the Lord as her personal Savior, she discovered the Bible. This motivated her. She began to study the alphabet immediately. Even as an older lady, she learned to read and write very well. Her study book was the Bible. How she loved it. She read and read. Her heart longed to know more and more about the Lord.

I trust that you have access to a Bible or that you have your own copy. In years past it was very difficult for many people in the former Soviet Union to secure a Bible. When we ministered at radio station Voice of the Andes in Ecuador, our Russian radio staff often offered to send a New Testament, a Bible, or other Christian literature to our radio listeners, but the books did not always arrive at their destination when we sent them.

I remember a letter that came to radio station Voice of the Andes from a group of woman who lived in a remote village in Russia. Their letter told us the following story.

In the quietness of their little homes in that remote village, these ladies began to hear the Gospel story while listening to their radio. The messages that they heard touched their hearts. One by one they knelt by their radio receivers, repented of their sins, and asked Jesus to come into their hearts. Talking together in the village, they soon discovered that their newfound faith in the Lord united them.

They began meeting secretly in different homes during the hour of the radio programs. They attempted to sing the songs that they had heard, and they were blessed and encouraged by the reading of God's Word and by all the sermons they were hearing. They eagerly joined in during the prayer time. But they had one sorrow. Not one of them owned a Bible. They had to have one. Where could they find one? This became a great trial to them. They were so eager to read God's book.

Finally they gathered some money together and sent the youngest lady on the bus to the nearest town in search of a Bible. After she had quietly questioned several people, someone gave this woman the address of a small House of Prayer located at the edge of the town.

Upon her arrival there, she approached the first man she saw. He was the pastor. She told him her story and in a whisper asked him, "Can you please tell me where I could buy a Bible?"

He looked around to see if anyone was listening. "There are no Bibles for sale in this town" he said. "We only have two copies among us. One of the families of the congregation borrows one of the Bibles during the week to read to his family. And I use the other one to prepare my sermons. We have no others."

The lady started to cry. "I cannot go back to my village without one. We are a small group of believers, and we need to have a Bible to learn more about the Lord."

By now it was time for the evening service to begin. This was the first Gospel service that this lady had ever attended. As the choir and the congregation sang, and as the pastor read the Scripture and prayed, this dear woman wept with joy. She was so blessed. When the service ended, those around her lovingly greeted her as a sister in the Lord. But soon they were all gone. Only the pastor and this lady were left standing in the back of the church.

"What shall I do?" she asked him sadly.

Just then the pastor's wife reentered the building. She put her arm around their guest and invited her to spend the night with them in their apartment.

After having their tea, the pastor invited them to pray together before they retired. "Dear Lord," he said. "You see the cry of this dear sister's heart. Please send her a copy of your Word so that she and the other dear ladies in her village can read it and learn more about You." Then they quietly went to rest.

In the morning she awakened to the music of the tea kettle and the aroma of fresh bread. Together the three of them thanked the Lord for a new day. Then they thanked Him for the food and quietly ate their breakfast.

Soon it was time for the visitor to catch her bus. Very slowly the pastor raised his eyes to meet hers. "Dear sister, I could hardly sleep last night," he said. "I prayed and prayed, asking God to send you a Bible. All I heard Him say was 'Give her yours.'"

Slowly, he lifted his Bible from the table and handed it to her. "Dear sister, I give you the greatest treasure I own. However, not only do I give you my own Bible, I give you the promise of our prayers. We will pray that through the testimonies of you ladies, many others in your village will find the Lord as their own personal Savior. And to prepare my sermons, I will share the only other Bible we have in our congregation."

With deep gratitude and with a choked-up voice she quietly said, "Thank you."

The pastor, his wife, and the visiting sister knelt to pray. Together they dedicated that Bible to be the instrument that would lead many others to Christ. She returned to her village with a big smile on her face and the Word of God safely tucked in her bag.

God speaks to us through His Word. As we read the Bible we are made aware of how much.

He loves us	Jeremiah 31:3
He helps us	Psalm 121
He comforts us	11 Corinthians 1:3-4
He understands us	Psalm 147:5
He supplies our needs	Philippians 4:13
He is everlasting	Psalm 106:1
He protects us	Psalm 121:7-8
He is good	Psalm 118:1
He has compassion	Psalm 103:13
He is our keeper	Psalm 121:5
He is our refuge	Psalm 46:1-2
He is our light	Psalm 27:1
He is our hiding place	Psalm 119:114
He leads me	Psalm 23:2
He is near	Psalm 145:18
He made us	Psalm 139:14-15
He gives us our desires	Psalm 37:4-5

God gives us a wonderful promise in Psalm 32:8. *I will instruct you and teach you in the way which you should go; I will counsel you with My eye upon you.* It is while we read His Word that God speaks to our hearts. And as God speaks to us, our hearts are warmed with His love, and we are blessed with His holy Presence.

I would like to finish this chapter with a very unusual story. It is a true story, written by a wonderful Christian author, Beth Moore. In her book, *A Woman's Heart,* she tells about the time her father served as an American soldier in Germany during World War II. He was in the battalion that broke through the gates of the Nazi concentration camp in Dachau, Germany. The Nazis had killed more than 41,000 people in this camp during the time of the Holocaust. Now these brave American soldiers were bringing freedom to hundreds of gaunt, weak, starving prisoners. As the soldiers entered the prison yard, many of the prisoners fell at the feet of their liberators with kisses and cries of gratitude. Now they were free!

In the midst of all the shouts of joy, they discovered a group of distraught children among the prisoners. For some, their parents had died. Others had been separated from their families, and they had no idea what had happened to them or where they were. They felt lost.

The American army immediately set up hospital-like care for them. They fed the children, bathed them, clothed them, and warmed them. They tried to make them as comfortable as possible. However, that did not prevent the nightmares and the restlessness which affected them so much that they could hardly sleep.

One evening a man went to the kitchen and got several loaves of bread. He lined up the children just before bedtime. He gave each child a piece of bread. Suddenly, their mood changed. Grasping their portion of bread, each child went to his bed and peacefully went to sleep. By holding bread in their hands, they knew that there would be food in the morning.

That story really touched my heart. In time, it became even more vivid. While I was doing missionary work among Slavic refuges in Frankfurt, Germany during 1950 and 1951,

I visited this same horrible internment camp in Dachau. It had only been six years since World War II had ended and since this concentration camp had been liberated. I walked through the damp buildings with their scarred walls and broken window panes. I felt the cold wind blowing around us. I saw the gas chambers where many thousands had died.

As I stood looking at the gas jets sticking out of the walls, I found myself trembling as I felt the horror of that room. In the yard I saw the huge dead tree with an extended limb where many prisoners had been hung. Our guide was convinced that the tree had died because of all the blood that had been shed there. What a sad place!

As I read the story of those dear, starving children, I was struck how very important bread had been to them. Just plain bread! Even as bread sustains our bodies, so Christ, the Bread of Life, sustains us and strengthens us through His Word, which then helps us grow spiritually.

Just think, as we read His Word and as we commune with Him, Who is the Bread of Life, we have the joy of His Presence with us. The Bible guides us, it counsels us, and it lifts our spirits.

We also learn how to grow in our faith. In Romans 10:17 it says, *So faith comes from hearing, and hearing* (or reading) *by the word of Christ.* Let us follow my Babushka Anna's example. Let us just read and read and read God's Precious Book!

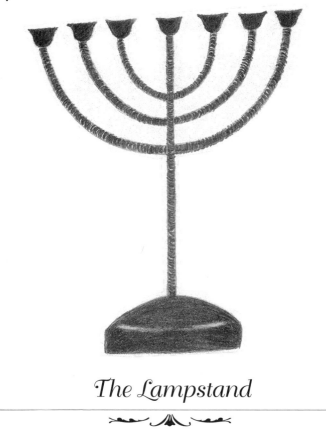

Chapter 9

The Lampstand

~~•∕ ⋀ ∖•~~

In the beginning God created the heavens and the earth.
Our earth had no shape or form. It was empty, and it was
completely DARK! But the Spirit of God was there, and God
simply said: *Let there be light!* Those words changed everything. Suddenly there was LIGHT! *God called the light day,
and the darkness He called night* (Genesis 1:1-5).

And light is also what the tabernacle needed. So God gave
Moses explicit instructions as to what kind of light he should
provide for the tent of meeting. It was to come from a golden
lampstand! That lampstand became the most exquisitely
beautiful piece of furniture in the tabernacle.

The lampstand was the first object that Aaron and his
priestly sons would see when they came into the Holy Place.

Standing along the south wall, it stood opposite the table of the bread of the Presence, and it shed light on the bread of the Presence. It gave light as the priests gathered around that table, where they fellowshipped with the Lord and ate the bread together. The lampstand also gave light to the altar of incense.

The lampstand was the only source of light in the tent of meeting. There were no windows in the Holy Place, no place where natural light could enter. Skins and fabrics covered over the tent to protect it, so it was very dark inside. The only opening into the Holy Place was through long, heavy curtains. They were pulled to one side to provide an opening only when Aaron and the priests entered. The curtains would immediately fall back into place, leaving the tent of meeting in darkness except for the seven burning lamps on the golden lampstand.

It was while Moses was upon Mount Sinai that God gave him explicit instructions as to how the lampstand was to be constructed. It was to be made of pure gold! Nor was any form or mold to be used. No, God said it was to be of hammered work, forming only one piece of solid gold.

Three branches were to extend from each side of the lampstand, with the shaft in the center making seven branches in all. On the top of each branch there was to be shaped an open almond flower with a cup nestled on top of each flower. These cups would hold the oil, so that when the wicks were lit, they would give out light. Probably flax or linen threads woven together were used as wicks in the oil lamps.

It is hard to imagine all the work that had to be done to make this lampstand. It needed to be shaped correctly. The gold had to be hammered into the very intricate shapes and precise forms that God had indicated. Only very skilled craftsmen could do such work (Exodus 25:31-40).

God told Moses that there should be seven lamps attached to the lampstand. He also told him to make the lampstand upright and to make sure that it reflected its light outward so that it would give off a strong light on everything before it. The snuffers and the trays that would be used alongside the lampstand were also to be made of gold. Once again, God reminded Moses to follow carefully each instruction that he had been given on the mountain (Exodus 25:37, 38).

There were further instructions from the Lord. *You shall charge the sons of Israel, that they bring you clear oil of beaten olives for the light, to make a lamp burn continually* (Exodus 27:20). Yes, it was the continual responsibility of the Hebrews to keep bringing a supply of clear olive oil for the lampstand. It was special oil, made from crushed unripen olives, which gave a nearly smoke-free light. It was very important that the lamp was always shining. This meant that a constant supply of olive oil was imperative.

Since the lamps had to burn continually, the priests had to watch over them carefully from evening till morning. It was important for them to keep replenishing the oil in the cups. As they attended the lampstand each evening, the Scripture also tells us that the wicks needed to be trimmed. The priests would take away the black carbon that would collect on the wick and place it on the golden pan and take it away. This would keep the flame burning clean and bright.

So we see that the lampstand was the only source of light for the Holy Place. By its light the priests placed fresh loaves on the table of the bread of the Presence. By its rays they could also replenish the incense on the altar of incense. By the lampstand's bright light the priests fulfilled the duties which God had given them! Indeed, Moses followed all of the instructions that God gave him! (Exodus 25:31-40, 26:35, 27:20-21, 30:8, 37:17-23, Leviticus 24:1-4).

Reflections of Divine Light!

Siberia! Four o'clock in the morning! Winter! There was a rapid knock on our train compartment door. Then the brusque voice of the train attendant: "Hurry, hurry, girls, we are arriving shortly. Bring your bags and stand by the door. You are the only passengers getting off in Venzilee. Be quick about it. We are already late."

My traveling companion, Svetlana, smiled and nodded her head. "Well, let us go," she said, as she dutifully untied and then unlocked our compartment door.

Svetlana and I had just participated in a two-day women's conference in Omsk, Russia. Over two hundred women had arrived from many towns, villages, and hamlets to attend that conference. After the first service I met two dear ladies who had travelled to the conference from the hamlet of Venzilee. "Oh, please, come and visit us, even for one day," they begged. "We have no church. We are just a small group of believers who gather in a home to worship the Lord. Many of us have listened to your radio programs for years," the women told us.

How could we say no?

And now, after a ten-hour journey, our train was coming to a jerking halt! Svetlana jumped off first and then turned to help me down the high step. It seemed that I had barely planted both feet on the ground when the train door slammed behind us, the train gathered speed, and was soon gone down the tracks and out of sight.

It was dark, cold, and the wind was blowing the scarf I had wrapped loosely around my neck. Nothing moved. We were alone, in the dark, in a Siberian hamlet!

As we tried to focus our eyes in the darkness, our gaze was suddenly drawn to a single naked light bulb swinging fiercely in the wind, high up on a pole alongside the dark, closed train station. "Let's head toward the light," said Svetlana.

We had to be careful where we walked, stepping over many sets of tracks. I would look down to see where to step and then look up intently for any light coming from that swinging bulb. As we got closer to the train station, we suddenly heard voices in the darkness calling out to us. "Ruth Petrovna, Svetlana! We are here."

We turned to the direction of their voices and saw another light. Now our friend's flashlight guided us toward them, and we were soon enveloped in their warm embrace.

We began our walk through the village. In the stillness of the night our feet made crunching sounds on the crisp snow. Suddenly I was aware of the mooing of cows and the crowing of roosters. Houses appeared, built of huge thick logs. Small barns were attached to the homes, permitting the animals to absorb some of the warmth that came through the walls of the houses. Our noise had awakened them.

Soon we arrived at the home of our hostess. There we soaked up the heat from the wood stove and appreciated the bright lights in her cozy two-room house. Oh, how we enjoyed the delicious tea which she served from her samovar.

Our service began about eleven o'clock in the morning. It was held at the home of another lady. Since she had eight children, her husband had built a larger home. All the Gospel services in the village were held in that house. Now many people gathered.

To our surprise the service and the warm fellowship continued most of the day. Some of the villagers there were hearing the Gospel for the first time. They listened with great intensity. We were so glad we had come!

Many years have passed since that visit to Venzilee. However, the experience remains a vivid memory in my heart. It was dark that night when we arrived, but the swinging light bulb gave us direction as we stumbled over the railroad tracks. The night was black, but the beam of our friend's flashlight guided us to them. Of course, those were only man-made lights.

But now we turn from that light swinging in the wind in Siberia to the divine light that comes from God Himself (I John 1:5). As King David said in II Samuel 22:29, *You are my lamp, O Lord; And the Lord illumines my darkness.*

Jesus said, "I am the light of the world."

Turning to the New Testament, we see Jesus on one of His visits to Jerusalem telling the people gathered there: *I am the Light of the world; he who follows Me will not walk in the darkness, but will have the Light of life* (John 8:12).

What a wonderful declaration! Jesus was not speaking about His teachings. Rather, He was speaking about Himself. He was explaining:

WHAT HE is: Jesus is THE LIGHT of the world!
WHO HE is: Jesus is THE LIGHT of men!
For WHOM is His light: For His followers in the world!
And the RESULT will be:
Jesus becomes THE LIGHT of our life!

Moreover, Jesus is the Eternal Light. In the first verse of the Gospel of John, we see that *In the beginning, was the Word, and the Word was with God, and the Word was God.* We clearly see that Jesus was at the beginning of all that exists.

This eternal Jesus entered our dark world to provide light and to provide spiritual life. How wonderful to know that Christ's true Light continues to shine in the midst of all the spiritual darkness that surrounds us. God's Light will prevail. John said, *In Him was life, and the life was the LIGHT of men* (John 1:4).

II Corinthians 4:4 tells us that Satan tries to blind the eyes of men so that they will not see the light of the Gospel. But we have this wonderful assurance: God is Light! God is holy, untouched by evil or sin. He alone can guide us out of the darkest sin into His heavenly light. As plants grow and flourish in the sunlight, so we can grow spiritually as we walk in His light.

In the Holy Place, the golden lampstand illuminated the table of the bread of Presence and the altar of incense. Now, today, it speaks to us of Jesus as the Light of the World! His divine light can illumine the dark minds of all men with truth and life!

In the Gospels we see how Christ's divine light attracted people. During Jesus' three years of public ministry here on earth, enormous crowds followed Him. Whenever Jesus saw the crowds, He felt love and compassion for them. Sometimes He would see people who were lame or sick, and He would heal them. He heard the cry of the man blind from birth, and He gave him sight. When He saw people who needed to be comforted, He would encourage them.

There were times when He saw that people were hungry. He fed thousands of them, to the amazement of His disciples. He spoke kindly to children and took them in His arms. His light brought them peace and joy.

Jesus said, "You are the light of the world."

But not only Jesus is to bring light to the world. When Jesus gave His Sermon on the Mount recorded in chapters 5-7 of Matthew's Gospel, one of the things He said to His disciples was: *You are the light of the world* (Matthew 5:14).

What a powerful statement! They had heard Jesus say, "I am the Light of the world." And they accepted that! But here was Jesus, seated beside His disciples, telling them that they were also the light of the world. What did He mean by this?

Jesus proceeded to explain, *You are the light of the world. A city set on a hill cannot be hidden; nor does anyone light a lamp and put it under a basket, but on the lampstand, and it gives light to all who are in the house* (Matthew 5:14-15).

In these verses Jesus used striking examples. He spoke of a city aglow in the night and of a lamp lighting a family home. But these examples were not only for the disciples sitting by Him in the countryside. These teachings are also for us today. Once we have repented, then the light of Jesus has entered our hearts. Remember, He clearly said, "You are the light of the world." Now He expects us to share that light with others.

Jesus goes on to explain that no one can hide the lights of a city set high on a hill. That is so true. I am reminded of my trip back to Quito, Ecuador, in 1995. It had been more than ten years since my last visit there. My heart was pounding with excitement as I looked through the window of the airplane. It was night time, and I was flying over the Andes Mountains, the second highest mountain range in the world. I knew that we should be nearing Quito. I was straining to see something, anything.

Suddenly, in the distance far ahead of us, I saw small, flickering lights. Quito! The city where I had lived for almost thirty years! The place where radio station Voice of the Andes was located. Abruptly, there she was--the city of Quito--high in the great Andes Mountains! I knew that I had arrived at my destination because I was seeing many, many shining lights! Nothing could hide them!

In another example that Jesus used, He says that if we put a cover over a light, it would then be a hidden light and could help no one. So, Jesus tells us to take our light and to put it on a lampstand. The lamp needs to be out in the open to fulfill its purpose. There it will give light to everyone in the house.

So Jesus tells us what we need to do. To be a true light in this world, we must live in such a way that His light will shine through us. We must shine like a beacon. Then everyone who sees us will know that we love Him. We will glow for Jesus!

We will have joy to share with others. We will love those who surround us. Our greatest desire will be to live only for Christ, to help those in need, and to tell them about our Lord. When we live for Christ, those who see us will also want to have a personal relationship with Him (Matthew 5:16).

Not that we ourselves should be glorified. No! But others will see the reflection of our Heavenly Father in our lives. They will be able to see that Jesus, the Light of the world, has come to live in our hearts.

Gone is our past life of spiritual darkness. Now we walk in the light. We commune with the Lord in prayer. We know that He speaks to us as we read His Word. We will reflect His light when we have an intimate relationship with Him.

If we are really desirous to know the Lord and to abide in Him, we need to be walking in the same manner as He walked. The Lord tells us to be holy even as He is holy! (I Peter 1:15-16). Light and darkness cannot exist together. When Jesus, the TRUE light, is shining in us, all of the darkness disappears. When we accept Jesus into our heart, His light shines through us.

However, I John 2:9-11 does give us a warning. *The one who says he is in the Light and yet hates his brother is in the darkness until now. The one who loves his brother abides in the Light and there is no cause for stumbling in him. But the one who hates his brother is in the darkness and walks in the darkness, and does not know where he is going because the darkness has blinded his eyes.*

Dear ladies, we must confess that this verse about love and hatred does not only refer to men. Sadly, we women can also be guilty of holding hatred in our hearts towards others.

Perhaps some lady says something very hurtful to us. We may vow never to forgive her. Or another lady passes us by without saying one word of greeting. We are hurt forever. We even vow never to speak to her again.

What happened to that light which we knew while we were walking in love with Jesus? Hatred for our sister has shut out Christ's light in our life. How important it is to let Christ's love guide our lives. Then we will never need to stumble in hatred and darkness. Rather we are walking in His Light.

I was invited to speak one Saturday to a large group of women in a Slavic church in the United States. We had a joyous time of fellowship. We sang and studied God's Word in both the morning and afternoon services. And who could forget the delicious meal that was prepared for all of us? It was a blessing to be there and to meet several ladies who had accepted the Lord beside their radio receivers while they were living in Russia.

At the end of that day, while I was talking with a dear sister, with tears she mentioned to me that one of the ladies of her church never attends any of the women's meetings. The sister talking with me had personally invited that disgruntled lady to come for this special day, but she would not. It seems that she did not like the young woman who was assigned by the deacons to lead the women's group in the church. Sadly, her dislike for that sister who was leading the meeting kept Christ's light from shining in her own life. Others felt the discord and were saddened by it as well.

Thank the Lord, as Christians we can live in harmony with one another. The Psalmist David said; *Behold, how good and how pleasant it is for brothers* [and sisters] *to dwell together in unity!* (Psalm 133:1). And when there is unity, Christ's light shines brightly.

It has been my great joy to meet with women in many countries of the world. The Word of God has been the center of our fellowship. I have seen the light of Jesus on their faces as they have testified. Our prayer times were always a blessing, even though I did not always understand their language.

Ruth Petrovna on the left and her new friends in Asia

In one Asian country where Christianity is often not welcome, I was invited to speak to a group of ladies during one of their weekly women's meetings. Upon entering the simple room, we took our shoes off and sat in a circle on straw mats, with our legs crossed. These ladies, dressed in their colorful long-flowing dresses, sang their songs of praise with joy in their hearts and with smiles on their faces. And, oh, how they prayed. My missionary friend translated my lecture into their language. They listened intently. They often nodded in agreement as I would quote a passage of Scripture.

When the service was over, several of the ladies came to thank me for visiting them. I made sure that my missionary friend was close by to translate. Then a lovely, smiling, young lady stood before me holding her baby son. She looked into my eyes and said, "I have only accepted Jesus recently. I had never heard about Christ before. My neighbor invited me to this women's group, and here I found Jesus. My husband is a Muslim and does not allow me to attend the church services on Sundays. I can only come to be with the women in their weekday services."

She looked down at her sleeping child and said, "Every morning when I feed my son, I tell him about Jesus. During the day as I carry him, I tell him about Jesus. When I put him to bed at night, I pray with him and tell him about Jesus. I will continually teach my son to love Jesus."

I did not understand her language. But I want to tell you, I understood the beautiful light of Jesus on her face.

How glorious to arise every morning and to ask Jesus to show us our daily footsteps. There is no other true light but God's Light! As we ask Him to lead us, the light of His Word will always show us the right path and will guide us to be a light in the dark world around us.

I want to tell you about others I have met who have been a "light" for Jesus!

*On one of my first trips to Ukraine, I met a lady who was very concerned about the widows in her church. She had organized a group of women to help her. Together they gathered funds, bought new fabric, and sewed a black skirt as a gift for every widow in their church. Their kindness was a light that brightened many widows that Christmas.

*I know a Babushka who always bakes a sweet-bread for her grandsons when they come to visit her from another town. She does this with such love.

*In Belarus I spent the night in the small home of a single lady who cares for her elderly mother. She showed me her very large vegetable garden and admitted that it was a lot of work. She was very tired.

When I suggested that she not plant so much, her answer was "Oh, but I must do it to have food to give to those ladies who are too sick or too elderly to have their own gardens."

*Several months ago I was travelling with brother Konstantine, a missionary friend of mine. After several special meetings, we were taking an airplane together to our home towns.

I got on the plane first. Brother Konstantine was behind me. When I got on, I simply said, "Hello," to the two stewardesses and walked on to my seat.

Those same stewardesses then greeted brother Konstantine. He in turn smiled and said, "God bless you!" I saw the shocked faces of those two stewardesses. They became so excited. They smiled such big smiles and thanked him.

Brother Konstantine and I sat down in our assigned seats. It wasn't long before those same ladies came to brother Konstantine, one with a pillow and the other with a blanket. Then they asked him if he needed anything else. They were very kind to him. They wanted to serve him the best they knew how. I saw their reaction to the light of Jesus in brother Konstantine when he simply said, "God bless you!"

*A light that I will always remember came through the dedicated lives of a brother and sister, Mary and Nicholai Beechick. They were the leaders of the youth in the Russian church that I attended in Chicago during my growing-up years. They faithfully cared for the spiritual life of us young people. The light of their example has stayed with me all of my life.

*I have a story from Russia. In the early 1990's a group of ladies from an evangelical church decided to show the light of Jesus in a practical way. They took their pails, soap, and rags and went to a local home-for-the-aged care center. They volunteered to wash the windows, the beds, and the floors at the center. They began to develop friendships with the elderly and helped them with personal care. Each time they returned to clean, they would bring fruit or special baked treats.

Soon the administration began to question them. "Who are you? Where are you from? We cannot pay you. Why are you doing this?" They simply smiled and told them they were doing this in the name of the Lord Jesus! Their light certainly shone brightly, and brought joy to many hearts.

None the less, I am sure some of you are still thinking: "What can I do and where can I go to share my light? I have no talents. I cannot sing. I am too old." Or maybe you are saying: "I am too young. I have no money. I have no idea where or how to start. Maybe someone else can do that." Let us see if we can give you a few suggestions.

How can I be a light for Jesus?

- *Visit someone who is lonely or someone who is sick.*
- *Show sympathy to someone who is having a problem.*
- *Give someone a hug and tell them that you love them.*
- *Offer to pray with someone who is having a problem or is carrying a burden.*
- *Share extra food from your garden with people in need.*
- *Offer to help a mother with many children, especially when there is sickness in the family.*
- *Thank the choir director, the pianist, and the choir members for their inspirational music.*
- *Visit someone who has not been in church for a while.*
- *Offer to help someone who is caring for a home-bound family member and who finds it hard to get away from his or her responsibilities.*
- *Be kind to children. Be sure to tell them that they are loved.*
- *Speak kindly to everyone in your family.*
- *Never go to bed angry with your children or your husband. Always be ready to ask forgiveness.*
- *Give people a smile. Let them know that you are happy in Jesus.*
- *Telephone someone and encourage them.*
- *Compliment children whenever they achieve something.*
- *Encourage the young people in your church.*
- *Thank your family when they help you.*
- *Tell someone: "God loves you!"*
- *Always reflect the light of Jesus to your family!*

We serve the Lord when we serve others. We are Christ's light on this earth! How brightly is our light shining?

Perhaps as the problems of life surround us, we may find that our own relationship with the Lord is ebbing. Have we allowed things to enter our lives that are not pleasing to Him? Is our own spiritual flame sputtering? Is our testimony not as bright as it should be?

Just as the priests in the tent of meeting had to trim the wicks on the seven lamps of the lampstand in the Holy Place, the wick of our own inner light often needs to be trimmed. We must read His Word. We must go to Him in prayer. As we commune with Him, He will cleanse us. He will take away the things that are hindering our testimony and are dimming His light in us.

I remember the visits that our family sometimes made to a Russian church in the state of North Dakota in America when I was a little girl. It was a farming community. Large families had emigrated there from Russia and Ukraine. My father was often invited there to preach at their conferences.

In the late afternoon I was fascinated to watch sister Tovstenko, the pastor's wife, while she diligently cleaned the black soot that had formed on the globe of their lamp. Then she would clean off the wick's black carbon and carefully trim the wick itself. When she finished this task, she would light the lamp and place it on the shelf. Suddenly, great light would burst across the darkening room while she filled the table with delicious food for our evening meal.

Now, today, we live in dark days. People lost in sin need to see the reflection of God's love in us. Let us ask the Lord to keep the flame and the radiance of His light in our own lives, so that those around us will see Jesus through us.

Do you want to grow spiritually? Keep the light of Jesus shining brightly in your life.

Taking His Light to the World

And He said to them, 'Go into all the world and preach the Gospel to all creation' (Mark 16:15).

He is not here, for He has risen (Matthew 28:6). These words changed the world! Three days after Jesus was crucified and His body was placed in a tomb, HE AROSE FROM THE DEAD! The world was changed forever!

After His resurrection, Jesus appeared many times to His disciples.

Each time they saw Him, they looked at Him with awe. He had died. Yet there He stood before them, their risen Lord and Savior.

For three years these men had walked the dusty roads with Jesus. He had spent hours and hours teaching them from the Scriptures. For three years they had seen the great miracles that He had performed. He had been their teacher, and they loved Him.

On one occasion after His resurrection, Jesus met with His eleven disciples on a mountain in Galilee. There He had a very serious conversation with them. He told them that with His resurrection came supreme authority. It was with this absolute authority that He now wanted to give them a very special message. And they listened! It was Jesus' great command: *Go therefore and make disciples of all the nations, baptizing them in the name of the Father and the Son and the Holy Spirit, teaching them to observe all that I commanded you* (Matthew 28:19-20).

We must remember that, until the time of His arrest, the disciples had all lived together as a tight-knit group. But now Jesus is telling them that He wanted them to "GO" to other nations and to TAKE HIS LIGHT TO THE WORLD! Not merely to the Jews in the area where they were living. They must now take the Good News of salvation everywhere, yes, even to the entire world. To the most far-away places! (Mark 16:15).

This message must be told to everyone that Jesus has already paid the penalty for their sin. Then those who repent of their sins and believe in Jesus will have their sins forgiven. And they will have eternal life with God!

This was Jesus' Great Commission!

• *WHAT was His command?*.................... *To GO to every creature*

• *WHERE should they go?* .... *To ALL the world*

• *WHAT should they do?* .... *PREACH the GOSPEL*

• *To WHOM?* .... *To ALL people*

When Jesus had finished giving this message to His disciples, He also promised them that He would always be with them. No, He was not sending them off alone. No matter where they would go to take the message of God's Word, Jesus would be with them.

Several days later Jesus brought His disciples together one more time on the Mount called Olivet. He knew that the hour had come for Him to return to His Heavenly Father. He wanted to give them some final words of instruction. Standing there on the Mount, His disciples heard Jesus say *. . . and you shall be My witnesses both in Jerusalem, and in all Judea and Samaria, and even to the remotest part of the earth* (Acts 1:8). Jesus was reminding them, yet one more time, to take the message of salvation to all the world!

When He had finished speaking, Jesus was lifted up into heaven. As His disciples gazed upward, they saw a cloud receive Him out of their sight.

When they could no longer see Jesus, two men in white clothing appeared beside them and said, *Men of Galilee, why do you stand looking into the sky? This Jesus, who has been taken up from you into heaven, will come in just the same way as you have watched Him go into heaven* (Acts 1:11). And with those encouraging words, the disciples returned to Jerusalem.

Upon their arrival in Jerusalem, the disciples immediately went to the upper room where they had been staying. There they joined other believers, including Mary the mother of Jesus, some of the other women who had followed Him, and His brothers.

And what did they do? Together, they wholeheartedly devoted themselves to earnest prayer. Yes, they prayed! (Acts 1:8-14).

The Great Commission that Jesus gave to His disciples in the New Testament is the same command that He gives to us who are His disciples today! Earlier we saw where Jesus said, *"You are the light of the world"* (Matthew 5:14).

Many, many people live in darkness today because they have never heard about Jesus and His love. The Great Commission tells us that because we are the light of the world, we must go and be His witnesses, taking His Light everywhere. "Go," said Jesus. "Go... to all the nations."

And many of His followers have obeyed the Lord's command. They have gone to very difficult places in this world. Let me tell you about a few who have taken the light of the Gospel to some very dark corners of the world.

Africa

My heart was deeply moved as I read about two Moravian men who went to Africa as missionaries. But this was not an ordinary mission station. They went to live in a leper colony.

This took place during the 1800's when there was limited medical help for those who were ill with leprosy. The story is told that those who were stricken with this dreaded disease in a certain area in Africa were forced to live in a specially designated enclosure. That place was surrounded by a high wall. There was adequate land for the patients to plant and cultivate gardens in order to have food.

However, there was no exit from this compound. Once a person entered through the gate, he was never allowed to leave the grounds again. Leprosy was a greatly feared disease. There was always the fear that this awful disease would spread to others. So they were never permitted to leave their high-walled area.

When the two Moravian men heard about this closed leprosy colony, they immediately thought about the souls of those people. How would these people ever be able to hear about the love of Christ? They were condemned to die behind that high wall without the knowledge of God. And they would never know of His great love.

It was then that these men made their decision. They would go to live with these lepers in order to be a witness to them. They would take the light of Jesus into that dark and hopeless colony. They would teach the lepers the Word of God, and that would give them hope.

But it also meant that these two men, themselves, would never be able to leave the colony. They would die there! Without hesitation the two missionaries left their friends and family and went to Africa to live, to witness, and to die among the lepers!

This story challenged my heart. I asked myself. "Would I be willing to do that? Would I be willing to go there? Do I love the souls of men that much?"

What amazed me even more was what I read at the end of this story. There were two other young Moravian men who greatly encouraged these new missionaries just before they left for Africa. These young men told them that should the Lord take them to heaven, they would go and take their place. They would continue taking the light of Jesus to that dreaded leprosy colony in far-away Africa!

Russia

Then there is another story. This one took place in Russia in the 1920's. Ivan Stepanovich Prokhanov tells us about it.

A young Christian girl, not yet twenty years of age, came to Brother Prokhanov one day seeking his advice. She felt that God was calling her to be a missionary among the Yakut people in faraway Siberia. She felt compelled to tell them about Jesus. Her friends tried to dissuade her. However, Brother Prokhanov gave her his blessing for this missionary work. "I cannot stand in the way of anyone who has received the command of Christ," he said.

It wasn't long before this young lady set off on her own across the northern marshes of Siberia and settled among the Yakut huts.

Nothing was heard about her for several years. Finally a letter arrived with incredible news. There were now many people who had repented and who had opened their hearts to the Lord. They wanted to be baptized. She called for men to come to baptize these people and to organize a church. The light of the Gospel and her love for God had shone through her life as she lived among them. All of this happened because this young lady listened to the voice of God and obeyed Him. Hers was the high honor of taking the Light of Jesus to the land of the Yakut people.

What a touching testimony. Here was a young Russian girl who felt God calling her to take the Gospel to the forgotten Yakut people and she went! In Isaiah 49:6 we read, *. . . I will also make you a light of the nations so that My salvation may reach to the end of the earth.* This young lady obeyed God's call to go to the people of Yakut. She became a light for Jesus.

As the people watched her life and heard her testimony about God's great love, many repented of their sins. They received God's forgiveness, and His glorious Light entered their lives also. Many are with the Lord today because this young Russian girl obeyed the call of God! Today God is still calling missionaries to go and serve Him. Who will go?

The South Sea Islands

From the past comes the amazing story of Mr. John Geddie, who was born in Scotland in 1815. Soon after his birth the Geddie family moved to Canada. After completing his basic studies, John Geddie chose to study theology. He was small in stature, and his health was not good. However, he told the Lord that if his health would be restored, he would preach God's Word at home or in far-away lands.

And God answered his prayer for good health. In 1838 he was ordained, became a pastor, and a year later was married. For seven years he preached to thousands of people in Canadian churches. But as he studied the Scriptures, he could not get away from the burden on his heart for those in faraway lands who had not heard the Gospel. Those heathen must also hear of God's love! He felt called of God to go to those who had not heard of Christ in the New Hebrides Islands (now called Vanuatu) in the South Pacific.

John and Charlotte Geddie and their children sailed from Halifax, Canada, on November 30, 1846. In his final message to his Canadian congregation, Geddie said, "In accord with the Redeemer's command and assured of His presence, we are going forth to those lands where Satan has established his dark domain. I know that suffering awaits me. But to bear the Redeemer's yoke is an honor to one who has felt the Redeemer's love."

After a journey of 20,000 miles, the Geddie family arrived in Pango-Pango, Samoa. There they spent six months learning the Samoan language.

Then they proceeded to the southernmost island of Aneiteum, landing there in 1848. As the ship that had brought them sailed away, the missionaries suddenly felt as if they were abandoned.

The residents of this island were known as barbarous people. They were cannibals. The men wore long hair and painted their faces in a hideous fashion. The women chopped their hair short and wore a girdle made of big leaves. The men went about almost naked. They were savages who killed unwanted babies. When a man died, his wife was strangled so their spirits would continue to be together.

Yet, in one of his letters to his friends at home, Geddie wrote, "We are not alone. We have His promise, at whose command we have come. 'Lo, I am with you always.'"

In another letter he said, "The love of Christ sustains us. My heart longs to tell this miserable people the wonders of Christ's redeeming love."

At that point in his life, he had not met one person on that island who had ever repented of his sin or who had ever invited Jesus to come into his heart.

The first thing the Geddie family did was to learn the Aneityuim language and to put it into writing. Then Geddie began to translate the Scriptures into the Aneityuim language. Schools were started to teach the natives to read.

The missionaries spent many hours in personal conversation with the people. Geddie preached to them about the love of God. In the beginning the men attended the church services with their faces painted and carrying their clubs and spears. As they began to hear the Word of God, these customs diminished. The islanders also began to cover themselves.

Geddie taught the islanders to read portions of the Bible as he continued to translate it. When they repented, he nurtured them and explained the teachings of Jesus. Geddie knew that he would leave the island someday and that those converts would need to continue spreading the Word of God themselves. He also took new Christians with him whenever he would go to preach on other islands.

Can you believe that in the six years after the Geddie missionary family arrived in Aneiteum, half of the population had come to a personal faith in the Lord Jesus Christ!

What rejoicing there was the day God answered one of his most earnest prayers. That was the day when Yakanui, a very wicked chief, came to Geddie. Yakanui wanted to know about God's forgiving love. Yakanui had been greatly feared and hated, for he was vicious and cruel. The missionary tenderly pointed him to the all-forgiving Redeemer.

What joy when Yakanui repented!

During their years on the island, John and his wife experienced many hardships and trials. John had to walk through the forests and over rough mountains to take the Gospel to other areas. Sometimes clubs and spears were hurled at him by the savages. Several times he was injured.

One of his greatest heartaches came the day that his three-year-old son, Alexander, became ill and died. But, always, he had a burning desire to continue taking the light of Jesus to these heathen people.

Geddie called for other missionaries from Scotland, who joined his family to help with the expanding ministry. There was so much work to do for the Lord. He completed the New Testament translation by 1860. Immediately he started the translation of the Old Testament, which he ultimately completed. Almost half of the population on the island became literate. Geddie kept encouraging and training the new believers to be Christian teachers and evangelists. Eventually, thousands of the savages left heathenism and turned to Christ. And in time, there were about twenty five churches established across several islands in that area.

John and Charlotte Geddie left the island of Aneiteum in 1872. What had motivated them to give twenty-four years of their lives to take the Gospel to the heathen savages on the island of Aneiteum and to other islands? John Geddie himself gave the answer. "My best enjoyments in time, and my prospects beyond the grave, center in the CROSS, which is the emblem of redeeming love."

God had called Geddie to go and tell those savages about the cross! Geddie obeyed the Lord! He went! And he served God faithfully!

John Geddie died in Canada on December 14, 1872. A special tablet was prepared in Australia and hung in a church on the island where the beloved missionary had preached for so many years. It reads:

"In memory of John Geddie, born in Scotland, 1815, Minister in Prince Edward Island (Canada) seven years, Missionary sent from Nova Scotia to Aneiteum for twenty-four years.

WHEN HE LANDED IN 1848, THERE WERE NO CHRISTIANS HERE:

WHEN HE LEFT IN 1872, THERE WERE NO HEATHEN."

The light of the Gospel that penetrated those areas is a wonderful example of the Scripture passage in Matthew 4:16, *The people who were sitting in darkness saw a great light and those who were sitting in the land and shadow of death, upon them a light dawned.*

We see that before John Geddie and his family arrived to the island of Aneiteum, or before the two Moravian missionaries went to the leprosy colony in Africa, and before the brave young Russian lady traveled to far-away, cold

Yakutsk, the inhabitants of those places walked in darkness because they did not have the light of the Gospel. It arrived to them through the life and the testimony of those missionaries who brought them the story of Jesus and the Cross! Who will follow their example?

The Birth of Slavic Gospel Association

Across the years, many other missionary pioneers obeyed the Lord's command to take the light of Jesus to those who were without the Gospel. One of them was my father, Peter Naumovich Deyneka. He burned with a passion to take God's Word to Slavic-speaking people around the world! To help realize this--after much prayer and fasting--he founded the Slavic Gospel Association in January 1934.

In those early years of SGA my father gathered funds to support Christian workers in Poland. He helped provide those workers with bicycles for transportation from village to village. In 1939 the first SGA missionary was sent to Alaska to minister to Russian-speaking Aleuts. In 1940 an SGA Russian missionary began ministry among Russians living in Cuba.

In November of 1940 my father was invited to South America. He spent four months in continual ministry among thousands of Slavic immigrants in Argentina, Uruguay, and Paraguay. He traveled and preached from one town to the next. The Lord sent deep conviction. Sinners repented. Christians were revived spiritually. Willful hearts were broken. Bickering church members, as well as church leaders themselves, begged God for forgiveness. What a revival!

On his way home to the United States, he stopped in Quito, Ecuador, to visit his friend, Clarence Jones. They were members of the same church in Chicago. Jones had recently established a missionary radio station called Voice of the Andes in Quito. Brother Jones asked my father to preach a sermon in Russian over the radio. Our family back home in Chicago was informed of the hour this would take place. It was March 1941. I was 13 years of age. At the appointed hour, we heard my father's voice come floating over the airwaves from Ecuador!

My father prayed, read Scripture, and preached. There in the city of Chicago we heard my father's voice coming from thousands of kilometers away! That was history! We are told that this was probably the first Russian sermon ever preached on the radio. Never did I imagine that someday I, too, would be giving the Gospel over radio station Voice of the Andes for almost 30 years!

Brother Jones encouraged my father to send Russian missionaries to Quito to begin regular Russian broadcasts. And my father did! Constantine and Elizabeth Lewshenia were the pioneers. Then my cousin, Alexander Leonovich, served there for over a year. Others followed!

Russian Gospel programs were beamed from Voice of the Andes for over 60 years, reaching Russian-speaking people in 87 countries with the story of Jesus! Other SGA Russian radio missionaries were also sent to Trans World Radio in Europe and Far East Broadcasting in the Philippines. Only in heaven will we know how many souls were saved from everlasting damnation because of the Gospel radio programs.

My father also had a vision to establish Russian Bible-training centers. He met with Oswald Smith, pastor of the Peoples Church in Toronto, Canada. When my father approached Pastor Smith with the idea of establishing a Russian Bible Institute in Toronto, he eagerly cooperated. SGA's Russian Bible Institute opened in Toronto in 1943. Its graduates went out as missionaries to Korea, the Philippine Islands, South America, Europe, Canada, and the United States.

Following the revival among Slavic people in South America, in 1944 SGA also established a Russian Bible Institute in Argentina. Hundreds of its graduates became pastors, missionaries, and Christian workers. Many new churches were established as people came to Christ. The fruits of this Bible Institute continue to this day.

Slavic Gospel Association has now celebrated its eightieth year of existence. My father's vision of training Russian Christian workers continues. Today, SGA sponsors four seminaries within the former Soviet borders, as well as several

Walter Covich, Ralph Bell, Dr. Oswald Smith, Peter Deyneka, Sr.

Bible Institutes. International Bible teachers and theology professors are sent periodically to teach the many students who are receiving Biblical training in various corners of the CIS, as well as in Israel.

One of the greatest cries from Russian people around the world that came to SGA was of their longing for the Word of God and for Christian literature. SGA has answered that plea by printing thousands upon thousands of Russian Bibles, New Testaments, song books, Bible Concordances, the Scofield Study Bible, and a popular diglot, the Russian-English New Testament and Psalms, as well as Billy Graham's book, *Peace With God.* Altogether, hundreds of titles have been printed. Each year more evangelistic books about missions, books on prayer, books for women, Bible doctrine, and many other titles, continue to be published. SGA is also helping produce a vast number of colorful Russian-language Christian works for children.

The children's books are especially well received through SGA's amazing children's ministries that are carried on in many areas across the former Soviet Union. The joy of Christmas has come to many a child who unexpectedly received a "gift bag." SGA's *Immanuel's Child* Christmas ministry is made possible by God's people, who send their offerings through SGA for the purchase of these gifts. Children of the community or local church, as well as those living in orphanages, are invited to hear the story of the birth of Jesus. They return home with an exciting gift, as well as beautifully illustrated children's literature.

Then there is the year-round ministry called *Orphans Reborn.* Pastors, church workers, and church youth hold weekly Bible studies in the local orphanages. They get to know and to love the children personally and to teach them God's Word.

Every summer SGA sponsors many camps for children and youth. There thousands of children hear the Gospel for the first time. And there they come face to face with Jesus during the camp sessions. Praise God, many have repented of their sins.

Today, SGA helps support hundreds of national missionary pastors as they plant churches. Some live in towns and villages where there were no believers when they arrived there. Many of these missionaries experience difficulties. But through their patient witness, people are finding Christ and churches are being established.

Also, in cooperation with the Children's Hunger Fund, food is delivered to many needy families. This opens doors for personal witness. As a result, many families are now attending Gospel services. Many have repented of their sins and have accepted the Lord.

Praise God that for over eighty years, the Slavic Gospel Association has been taking the light of the Gospel to people around the world. Many have come to know Christ as Lord and Savior.

Long ago, in the Old Testament tabernacle the lampstand sent out its bright light in the Holy Place.

In the New Testament, Jesus revealed Himself as the true Light of the world.

And, today, by that same light we can grow spiritually. Let us take this glorious light and proclaim His Gospel to all people!

Chapter 10

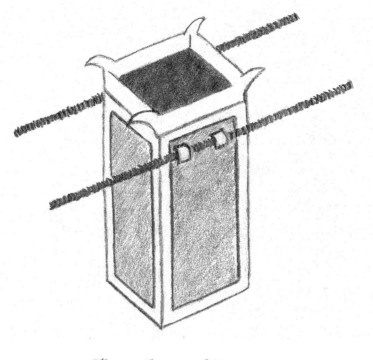

The Altar of Incense

~~~~~~⟋⟍~~~~~~

The last article of furniture to be constructed for the tabernacle's Holy Place was the altar of incense. There it stood: both the tallest article of furniture in the Holy Place and the smallest in size. It was to be built as a square with horns on each corner. The horns, as well as the altar itself, were to be made of acacia wood. All four sides of the altar, its top, and its horns were to be completely overlaid with pure gold.

Furthermore, a strip of gold molding was to be placed around the entire top edge of the altar of incense. Lower down there were four golden rings into which poles could be inserted for easy carrying wherever the Israelites traveled on their long journey to the Promised Land. These poles were also to be made of acacia wood and were to be overlaid with gold (Exodus 30:1-5).

Once a year Aaron was to perform a ceremonial cleansing of the altar of incense with blood from the sin offering for atonement. This blood was sprinkled on the horns of the altar (Exodus 30:10).

The Lord gave Moses specific instruction concerning the placement of the altar of incense. It was to be set directly in front of the veil which separated the Holy Place from the Holy of Holies. With the glorious reflection of the golden lampstand from the left side of the Holy Place and with the table of Presence on the right side, the altar of incense could be seen centered in front of the veil.

This position was very important, for on the other side of that veil, also centered, stood the ark of the testimony on which was placed the mercy seat. It was at this mercy seat that God's presence dwelt. And about that mercy seat, the Lord made this statement, *where I will meet with you* (Exodus 30:6).

If we could have been there, what we would have noticed most about the altar of incense would have been the overwhelming fragrance that arose from it by day and by night. The Lord gave very specific instructions about this incense. It was to burn continuously. He also gave Moses the precise names of the four spices that were to be used to make that special incense: stacte, onycha, galbanum, and pure frankincense.

Equal amounts of each of these exotic spices were to be combined together. Once all of these spices were well-blended, the result became a perfume which was both sweet and powerful, extremely fragrant, and very out of the ordinary. For the Lord had said, *you shall make incense, a perfume...salted, pure, and holy. You shall beat some of it very fine* (Exodus 30:35-36).

However, God made it clear that this very special mixture of spices was never to be used for personal enjoyment (Exodus 30:37). God also indicated that no other type of incense was ever to be burned on the altar. Only God's own special incense recipe was to be used in the tabernacle.

There were further instructions for Aaron, the High Priest. Each morning and each evening he was to go into the Holy Place and pour fresh, sweet-smelling incense on the burning coals of the altar of incense. Imagine how this pleasing, fragrant aroma must have blessed the Holy Place. As the Lord had said, *There shall be perpetual incense before the Lord throughout your generations* (Exodus 30:8). Jehovah was telling Moses that this ritual must be done from generation to generation.

At the same time as he poured fresh incense, Aaron was also told to examine the wicks of the seven lamps that were burning on the lampstand. He had to trim them faithfully each morning and each evening so that they would produce a bright light all day and all night.

No matter how busy Aaron might have become, he followed these instructions very faithfully. Indeed, this wonderful aroma also filled the Holy of Holies where the Lord had told Moses, *There I will meet with you...and I will speak to you* (Exodus 25:22). And that aroma was carried on high as a continuous cloud of incense before the Lord.

For the Israelites themselves, the altar's aroma of sweet fragrance was a symbol of their prayers and of their worship rising up to God. The altar was to be a reminder for them to give continual praise, adoration, and petition to Jehovah. Indeed, God Himself longed for His dwelling to be a place where His beloved people would fellowship with Him in prayer.

Now here we are today, thousands of years later. Our Heavenly Father still longs to have fellowship with us, His children. He longs to hear our petitions and our words of adoration. However, today we no longer need an altar of wood or stone. We do not have to bring animals to be sacrificed, nor do we need to burn incense as the Israelites did.

Why do we say this? It is because God's Son, Jesus, has now become the great sacrifice for our sins. He did this by dying on that cruel cross on Calvary. Then on the third day after His death, CHRIST AROSE! Forty days later Jesus ascended to His Father in Heaven. Now, there He sits at the right hand of God, ever making intercession for us (Hebrews 7:25).

While Jesus lived on this earth, we remember the many, many hours He spent teaching His disciples and His followers. His disciples watched Him, and they realized that His power was from God. They also saw how often He would go off to pray. Inspired by what they saw, they asked Him to teach them to pray. So Jesus gave them this model prayer, recorded in Matthew 6:9-13. He said, *Pray, then, in this way:*

"Our Father who is in heaven,
Hallowed be Your name.
Your kingdom come. Your will be done, on earth as it is in heaven.
Give us this day our daily bread.
And forgive us our debts, as we also have forgiven our debtors.
And do not lead us into temptation, but deliver us from evil.
For yours is the kingdom and the power and the glory forever.
Amen."

In the very beginning of this prayer Jesus encourages us to approach God with confidence and to call Him our Father! *Our Father who is in Heaven!* God is the Heavenly Father of all those who truly believe in Him: those who have repented of their sins. Jesus goes on to say, *I and the Father are one* (John 10:30), and *Whatever you ask in My name, that will I do so that the Father may be glorified in the Son* (John 14:13).

Prayer is communicating with God! When we awaken in the morning, how wonderful it is to thank the Lord for a good night of rest. That is what the Psalmist did when he said, *I lay down and slept; I awoke, for the Lord sustains me* (Psalm 3:5).

And as also we lie down at night for our rest, it is good to thank Him for His faithfulness to us all day long. Another time the Psalmist wrote, *The Lord will command His lovingkindness in the daytime; And His song will be with me in the night, a prayer to the God of my life* (Psalm 42:8). Always it is good to praise Him.

When we pray, we are meeting with our Lord. Time spent with God is the time when we get to know Him better. It is the time when we learn to love Him more and more. Jesus tells us, *when you pray, go into your inner room, close your door and pray to your Father who is in secret, and your Father who sees what is done in secret will reward you* (Matthew 6:6).

God longs to commune with us. And we can pray anywhere. It can be in a room, in a church, or some corner, or any area where it is quiet, where we can be alone with Him. And how many thousands of prayers at this very moment are going up to the Lord from hospitals, from prisons, or from people who are flying through the air or sailing over the ocean? Or even from someone in a forest at the edge of the city of Moscow! Let me explain.

I met Sasha, a young man who grew up in Moscow. His parents were not religious. He had never heard anything about God. He had never even seen a Bible. One lovely Sunday afternoon in the fall he took the bus to the end of the line in Moscow for a walk through the forest. The birds were singing. The sun was shining upon the branches of the brightly-colored fall leaves, leaves that seemed to be chattering together or clapping their hands.

Suddenly he stopped. He looked up and was overwhelmed with all the beauty surrounding him. He dropped to his knees and looked into the heavens. His thoughts were in a whirl. "Is there a God? Is there a Creator? Who could have made such beauty? I must find Him." While he was returning home on the bus, those questions kept repeating themselves in his mind over and over again.

It wasn't long before God answered his cry. One day Sasha met a gentleman who invited him to attend his House of Prayer. There he heard about the love of God. And there He met the Great Creator, the all-powerful, all-knowing, and all-wise God! Sasha repented of his sins and accepted the Lord into His heart.

When he finished telling me his story, Sasha said quietly, "You know, Ruth Petrovna, I sought the Lord in the forest. And I found Him! I have often returned there to pray and to commune with Him. And always I have thanked Him!"

Yes, we can pray or commune with God, any day, any hour, and anywhere. Remember these words? "I am with you always," said the Lord, "Even to the end of the age."

He waits for us to ask Him for help. *Ask, and it will be given to you*, He said, *seek, and you will find; knock, and it will be opened to you* (Matthew 7:7-8, 28:20).

We are also reminded that, *If I regard wickedness in my heart, the Lord will not hear* (Psalm 66:18). Sin hinders prayer!

We cannot expect answers to our prayers unless we have a clean heart.

But, prayer hinders sin! Just as Aaron and the priests needed to be cleansed at the laver before entering the Holy Place in the tabernacle, so must we seek cleansing for any sin within us. Scripture says, *the prayer of the upright is His delight* (Proverbs 15:8). Jesus reminds us that we need to abide in Him. He said, *If you abide in Me, and My words abide in you, ask whatever you wish, and it will be done for you* (John 15:7).

It is good to desire to grow spiritually. The more we commune with Him in prayer, the deeper we will go in our walk with God. The more we reach out to Him, the closer He becomes to us. The closer we feel His presence, the more we will realize our need of complete dependency on Him. His Word is full of instructions for us to accomplish all of this. If we are walking with God in prayer, we will be growing! II Peter 3:18 tells us, *but grow in the grace and knowledge of our Lord and Savior Jesus Christ.*

I read the life story of a missionary who lived in a heathen country far from his homeland. Every morning when he would awaken he would sing the Doxology!

Praise God from whom all blessings flow.
Praise Him, all creatures here below.
Praise Him above, ye heavenly host.
Praise Father, Son, and Holy Ghost.
Amen

After praising the Lord in song, this missionary would then kneel and pray. During this first prayer time of the day, he would ask the Lord to cleanse his heart and to make him a useful witness on that day. What a wonderful way to begin each morning, communing with the Lord!

Prayer is conversation with God! When we pray we can open our hearts to Him, as to a dear Friend. We can tell Him how we feel. Is our heart full of joy? Or are we experiencing sadness and pain? We can pause and open our hearts to Him for five minutes, or for an hour. He sits on His Throne of Majesty, patiently waiting for us to come to Him with everything that is upon our hearts. Everything! Nothing is too big, or too little. What a blessing to have a close relationship with our Lord.

The Lord tells us, *I have loved you with an everlasting love; therefore I have drawn you with lovingkindness* (Jeremiah 31:3). Imagine, our dear LORD actually tells us, "I HAVE LOVED YOU WITH AN EVERLASTING LOVE." He is the dearest Friend we can have on this earth. I love to sing this hymn.

Sing it with me.

What a Friend We Have in Jesus

What a friend we have in Jesus,
All our sins and griefs to bear!
What a privilege to carry
Everything to God in prayer!
Oh, what peace we often forfeit,
Oh, what needless pain we bear,
All because we do not carry
Everything to God in prayer!

Have we trials and temptations?
Is there trouble anywhere?
We should never be discouraged—
Take it to the Lord in prayer.
Can we find a friend so faithful,
Who will all our sorrows share?
Jesus knows our every weakness;
Take it to the Lord in prayer.

Are we weak and heavy-laden,
Cumbered with a load of care?
Precious Savior, still our refuge—
Take it to the Lord in prayer.
Do thy friends despise, forsake thee?
Take it to the Lord in prayer!
In His arms He'll take and shield thee,
Thou wilt find a solace there.

Recently I read a remarkable testimony written by Joni Eareckson Tada. She writes about her acquaintance, Diane. It seems that this young lady, Diane, has a very close relationship with the Lord. She has been stricken with multiple sclerosis. Her body functions have slowly deteriorated to the place where she now has to be fed by others because her fingers are curled and rigid. Her voice is barely a whisper. She is paralyzed.

Every morning Diane's friend Connie comes into her room to begin the long routine of taking care of her daily needs. The first thing she asks Diane is, "Are you ready to get up yet?" Usually her answer is, "No...not yet."

So Connie leaves the room quietly and shuts the door. Diane slightly turns her head on the pillow and looks up at the board hanging on the wall right beside her bed. Her eyes look up at pieces of paper and cards with the names and photos of many people. And then she begins to pray! Every morning Diane lovingly prays for each person by name.

She also prays for others who are bedridden. She prays for the elderly who are lonely and forgotten. She prays for the gangs on the streets and for youth who are lost without Christ. She prays for faithful missionaries serving the Lord around the world, and she prays for broken families. She lovingly brings many requests to the Lord. And she does this every day!

Diane does not want to be put in her wheelchair for the day until she has finished praying for every one whose name she has on her wall. She is not in a hurry. This is a most important time of the day for her! It is her personal, intimate time with her Lord. This is when she talks with Jesus, with whom she feels so close. Yes, she has physical limitations. But God accomplishes His will in her life as she faithfully communes with Him.

And I am sure this time spent talking to God is also what gives her strength and peace to accept the circumstances of her own physical incapacities. What a remarkable testimony! Diane's caring heart and her close relationship with the Lord are wonderful examples for all of us.

Indeed, the Lord wants us to tell Him all our sorrows and all our joys. There is no heartache too little that we cannot tell Him. He wants to hear our dreams, our thoughts, and our desires. He waits for us to tell Him what is in our hearts. In return, He tells us, *I am the Lord your God, who upholds your right hand, Who says to you, Do not fear, I will help you* (Isaiah 41:13).

I love to read Isaiah 40:11. There we see the prophet Isaiah referring to our Lord as a shepherd. *Like a shepherd He will tend His flock, In His arm He will gather the lambs and carry them in His bosom; He will gently lead the nursing ewes.* I am so encouraged when I read that our dear Shepherd carries us in His bosom. He holds us close to His heart. And the Good Shepherd also gently leads and cares for the young as well as the old.

Our prayers are like the incense that was placed upon the altar of incense. That wonderful aroma goes up and up, reaching our Heavenly Father! He is worthy of our praise. He longs to hear our prayers. He desires to answer our petitions. So why do we try to do things in our own strength? Why?

I am reminded of the day my son John, his wife Maria, and his young daughter Katrina came for a visit. I was talking to Maria and made this statement, "I do not know what I am going to do about that!"

Just then from the corner of the room came the voice of my little granddaughter Katrina. "Well, Baba, what about the Lord?"

I was astounded at her statement. Here was a ten-year-old little girl, taught by her parents, reminding me that I should be asking the Lord for the answer to my problem! Jesus said, *If you ask Me anything in My name, I will do it* (John 14:14). Katrina was so right.

God answers the prayer of faith! What better assurance can we have that God will answer our prayers than this verse: *And all things you ask in prayer, believing, you will receive* (Matthew 21:22). We must pray with faith. We must believe that God will answer our prayers according to His will.

He welcomes our petitions. His Word invites us to: *draw near with confidence to the throne of grace, so that we may receive mercy and find grace to help in time of need* (Hebrews 4:16). Access to the throne of God is our privilege through prayer. Scripture tells us, *ask in faith without any doubting* (James 1:6).

Here I must tell you a little story I read. It took place in a farming community in the Midwestern area of the United

States. It had not rained for a long time, and the farmers were beginning to worry about their crops. If it did not rain soon, they were afraid of losing their harvest.

The pastor of the local church decided to call a special prayer meeting. He knew that the congregation needed to pray together for rain. As the people gathered he saw their solemn faces. At the appointed hour the pastor arose before his sad congregation.

He could not help but notice an eleven year old girl sitting in the front row. But she was not sad. She was happy! There she sat with a big smile on her face. But something else caught his attention. By this young girl stood a bright red umbrella! Then the pastor himself smiled. The rest of the congregation had merely come to pray. This little girl came to pray in faith! And she expected to see God answer those prayers! She expected the rain to come! She brought her umbrella!

Devote yourselves to prayer! Those are the words that the Apostle Paul gives to us in Colossians 4:2, *Devote yourselves to prayer, keeping alert in it with an attitude of thanksgiving.* We are encouraged to live with an attitude of thankful prayer. All day long as we go about our daily tasks, we need to be aware that the Lord is always by our side.

For example, how many times I have lost my keys. Has that ever happened to you? I look everywhere and cannot find them. Then, suddenly, I remember the Lord. I stop to pray: "Lord, please help me find my keys."

Almost at once I find them, and I thank Him! He was there already by my side, just waiting for me to call on Him.

And mentioning keys, I read this statement. "Prayer is like a key that unlocks God's answer to our prayers."

We need to commit ourselves to live in an attitude of prayer and thankfulness for His loving presence and care.

I Thessalonians 5:16-18 shows us how we should do this.

Verse 16: *Rejoice always;* Begin by rejoicing. Look at things with a happy heart. Have a good attitude. Let your face show the joy of Jesus in your life!

Verse 17: *pray without ceasing;* Just like we breathe continually, we should be in the attitude of prayer continually. Pray with a joyful heart. Don't give up. Keep a praise to the Lord in your heart. Just keep praying!

Verse 18: *in everything give thanks; for this is God's will for you in Christ Jesus.* Look forward to your prayer time. Give thanks for everything. Thank Him for the little things. Not only for the big things, or for the good things. Accept God's will for your life, no matter what it is. Even if we do not understand it, have a thankful heart. Just trust Him! Remember, God knows the future. We do not!

Several months ago I attended a conference. Missionaries from faraway countries gave their testimonies. My heart was especially stirred as I listened to a pastor from India. He told us about the deep poverty, the many illnesses and the hopeless situations of his people. With deep faith, this pastor and his helpers are faithfully preaching the Word of God in that needy area. Praise the Lord, people are coming to Christ. Many are repenting of their sins.

This Indian pastor then told us that the first thing that the pastors in his country do for new believers is to encourage them to read God's Word and to pray. They make sure that each new convert joins a prayer group. The new believers are taught to pray with their families at home. They are encouraged to choose a friend and pray together.

Then he made this statement. "Prayer is the greatest weapon we can have. Prayer is changing the outlook of people in India. The Christian poor are trying to help themselves and to help each other. One of them said, 'We see that if we pray, it spreads.'"

How true! As we see God answering our prayers, we are encouraged to keep on praying and praying. That is how we grow in the Lord.

Recently, I read that a man approached Billy Graham and asked him what was the secret of the success of his great crusades?" Billy Graham simply answered. "There are three secrets. PRAYER, PRAYER, PRAYER."

Let me illustrate. It was in 1949 that a group of Christian men sent Billy Graham an invitation. Would he come to their city of Los Angeles, California, and hold some meetings? Brother Graham had already been holding meetings in other cities, and people were coming to Christ. But now this group of men was inviting him to hold a three-week crusade in their big city of Los Angeles. They promised to erect a huge tent for this crusade. A tent that would seat thousands of people!

As was his custom, Billy Graham turned to the Lord in prayer. In a letter to the secretary of the committee, Billy Graham wrote: "Let's go forward by prayer." In response many churches and pastors organized prayer groups for the crusade.

During this time in his life Billy Graham was also active in the ministry of Youth for Christ. It was while he was attending Youth for Christ prayer meetings held during Youth for Christ summer conferences in Indiana, Billy Graham became acquainted with my father, Peter Deyneka. My father was leading many of those prayer meetings.

Now, remembering my father's passion for prayer, Billy Graham contacted my father. He invited him to travel to Los Angeles just before the crusade was to begin. For several days Billy Graham and my father prayed together. They earnestly sought the Lord for His blessing on the meetings. Billy Graham was very aware that without the blessing and power of God upon his ministry, there would be little of eternal value accomplished.

God heard and answered their prayers! Tens of thousands of people came to Christ. Yes, prayer was the secret for the reason why so many people repented of their sins at Billy Graham's many evangelistic meetings around the world.

Situations may arise where we feel uncertain about knowing God's will. There are times when we have no idea how to approach a certain matter or how to pray for it. Within ourselves, we do not have the answer. But we do have a helpful verse in Romans 8:26 where we read, *In the same way the Spirit also helps our weakness; for we do not know how to pray as we should, but the Spirit Himself intercedes for us with groanings too deep for words.* Have you ever experienced what the Apostle Paul was writing about in the verse we just read? I certainly have.

Let me explain. There have been times when I have carried a heavy burden. I did not know how to pray about it. I could not even express it to myself, it was so painful. I would awaken out of a deep sleep with a heavy heart. There would be tears. In my stress I would pray once more, begging Him to help me with that problem and to show me His will. Only then would I be able to go back to bed and fall asleep. I could feel His peace flowing over my distraught heart. Yes, our Lord is a prayer-hearing and a prayer-answering God!

Across the years I have been blessed with what my Papa (Peter Naumovich Deyneka) wrote about prayer in his book *Much Prayer Much Power*. Here is one paragraph from his book.

> "Praying is simply talking to God from your heart and directing your thoughts and words to Him. God talks to us as we read the Bible; we talk to Him as we pray. Both are very important. Prayer is just like talking to a friend. It is not necessary to prepare a great speech. God understands us in our simplicity and desires to hear from all of His children."

We are constantly faced with making decisions. We need to pray and ask God to show us the right path. If we start off on our own, we will surely make mistakes. Rather, we need to ask Him, "Lord, What should I study? What school should I attend? Where should I go? What is your will for my life? Whom should I marry? Heavenly Father, please show me YOUR way. Guide me. Help me."

There is one verse in the Bible which my Papa quoted over and over again. I can close my eyes, and hear him repeating it yet. *Call to Me and I will answer you, and I will tell you great and mighty things, which you do not know* (Jeremiah 33:3).

Also, there is a phrase my Papa repeated over and over again. "MUCH PRAYER - MUCH POWER! LITTLE PRAYER – LITTLE POWER! NO PRAYER – NO POWER!"

What is the secret of knowing God's will for our lives? The Lord tells us that we must simply go to Him in prayer! We must call on Him. There He tells us that He will answer us and show us great and mighty things! Things we could not have even imagined! If we want true happiness and peace, we must listen to Him closely and follow His plan for us.

Prayer is made up of our asking, listening, and receiving. There is nothing either too small or too large for us to speak to the Lord about. In Philippians 4:6 we read, *Be anxious for nothing, but in everything by prayer and supplication with thanksgiving let your requests be made known to God.*

This is a wonderful promise from the Lord. It has helped me many times. Let me illustrate.

How well I remember the early days of our arrival in Ecuador to begin our work at radio station Voice of the Andes. Our son Vanya was just four weeks old. Everything was new and strange to us. But our hearts were joyful as we began our radio ministry. God had called us to serve Him there, and we were so happy finally to be in Quito!

Two weeks had gone by since our arrival when I noticed tiny sores on Vanya's cheeks. Since he was a strong, big baby, always happy, smiling, and growing well, I was not too concerned. I kept applying various creams. Months went by. Then suddenly Jack and I realized that these sores were not healing. Every morning Vanya's sheet was bloody because he would scratch the area of his sores during the night. Soon we knew that Vanya's condition was serious and that we would have to take him to the doctor.

Even on the bus as I took him to the skin specialist, I realized people were staring at Vanya's cheeks. Once we were in the doctor's office, he looked our son over, and quietly asked several questions.

"Did he have any sores before you arrived in Quito?"

"No, señor."

"When did the first sore appear?"

"On the second day after we came here."

"How long ago was that?"

"Almost a year ago."

After a short pause the doctor said, "I think your child is allergic to Quito's high altitude. His condition is serious. I suggest you leave Quito immediately. Otherwise he will continue to develop more of these on other areas of his body. Obviously, the high altitude does not agree with him."

Alarmed, I returned to our apartment with a heavy heart. When I told Jack the doctor's diagnosis, he became very quiet. The next three days I noticed that he fasted. He spent hours in prayer in between recording his radio programs. I also prayed as I gently washed Vanya's cheeks.

We prayed together. We asked our coworkers to pray. We asked God to please heal our son, if it was His will. We were so blessed in our work. Certainly we did not want to leave the radio ministry in Quito. We were so happy to be serving Him there, and surely we longed for our Vanya to be a healthy little boy.

Early the fourth morning after our visit to the doctor, as I went to pick up Vanya (who was making happy noises in his basket) I noticed the sheet was clean. The scabs had all fallen off. His cheeks were pink. The sores were gone. Vanya was healed!

Yes, we had been so anxious and concerned. But God had heard our prayers! He had healed our son! Oh, how we praised Him and thanked Him. And now we knew that we could continue in our radio ministry at Voice of the Andes in Quito. With the Lord's help, we did that for almost thirty years!

I am sure that you, too, have been encouraged through answers to prayer in your life. Have you noticed that every time we experience an answer to prayer, we feel more closely drawn to God? Somehow, our faith becomes stronger. We have felt His hand upon our lives. He has heard our cry. And He has answered! Praise His name!

When Jesus walked among us on earth as a man, He felt the need for constant prayer. *But Jesus Himself would often slip away to the wilderness and pray* (Luke 5:16).

In Matthew 14:23 we read that after Jesus finished serving the crowds and healing their sick, He sent His disciples away. Then, bidding the crowd farewell, Jesus went up on a mountain alone to pray into the deep night hours.

Then there was also the occasion when the scribes and Pharisees were angry with Jesus and were plotting to do evil against Him. And what did Jesus do? *It was at this time that He went off to the mountain to pray, and He spent the whole night in prayer to God* (Luke 6:12). The whole night!

Just as prayer sustained Jesus, prayer will sustain us!

Luda lives in a small village in the Chernobyl region of Ukraine. She lives in very harsh conditions in a little cottage.

She has a son who is in poor health and who has a difficult character. Fortunately, they have access to an open piece of land close to her cottage. There she spends many hours working in her garden, which gives her some access to food.

In the region where she lives, everyone knows Luda as "the woman who knows God."

When people meet her on the road and look into her eyes, they see a brightness that springs from the hope which she has in the Lord. For her, the cares of this life are very pale in comparison to the joy of the Lord that she holds deep in her heart.

Several summers ago there was a major drought in the area where she lives. Soon there were many fires in the surrounding area, fueled by the dry fields all around the country side. Suddenly, one of the fires began moving toward the village where Luda lived. The only hope that the villagers had to escape the flames was a narrow two-lane road that was between the village and the rapidly approaching fire. Winds came up. There was great fear in the village. They knew that the fire would soon cross the road, and everything they had would burn.

Some of the villagers ran to Luda's cottage. "Luda, Luda," they shouted. "Fire! There is a fire! You know God! Come! Pray! Ask God to stop the fire, or our village will burn up."

Luda joined the others as they ran towards the dirt road. As soon as she got there, she fell on her knees in the middle of the road. The fire was getting closer and closer. Luda began to pray! She asked God to please stop the fire so that their village would not be destroyed. "Oh, Lord! Please help us," she cried out.

As Luda prayed, suddenly the fire turned and began to burn in another direction. The village was saved! Now, the neighbors were ecstatic. God had answered Luda's prayer!

As Luda arose from her knees, with tears streaming down her face, she thanked God for hearing her prayer. She then turned to the villagers, who were all rejoicing. She began to tell them about her Lord. They quieted down and listened. She testified of the marvelous gift of salvation that God has offered to all who will believe in Him. Then she reminded them that they had just witnessed an example of His love and care for those who trust in Him. Yes, God had answered her prayer! He had saved their village!

When we trust in God, even in our most difficult circumstances, He hears our prayers. He responds to our cry. Yes, our earnest prayer rises before Him like sweet incense!

Dear Lord, *May my prayer be counted as incense before your face!* (Psalm 141:1).

Prayer
For me, to pray continually,
Is the same as to breathe constantly.
Lord, I long to speak to you from my heart,
To commune with You at all times!
(Vera Kushnir)

Chapter 11

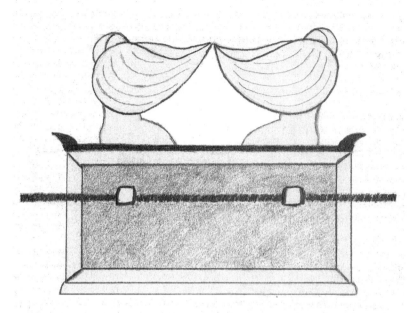

The Holy of Holies

Scripture tells us that on the day that the tabernacle was completed, the glory of the Lord filled the tabernacle. *Now on the day that the tabernacle was erected the cloud covered the tabernacle, the tent of the testimony, and in the evening it was like the appearance of fire over the tabernacle, until morning* (Numbers 9:15). It must have been awe inspiring!

Appropriately, the most holy place of that tabernacle was called the Holy of Holies. It was there that the Ark of the Covenant stood! Moreover, the Holy of Holies was where God Himself was present among His people.

The Holy of Holies was located just beyond the Holy Place, behind the heavy veil at the far end of the tabernacle. Its very name, Holy of Holies, tells us that this was the tabernacle's most sacred place. It was a sanctuary especially designed for God's glorious presence. The Ark of the Covenant was the only furniture in the Holy of Holies. It is interesting that the entire area of the Holy of Holies formed a perfect cube.

The partition between the Holy Place and the Holy of Holies was a heavy veil. That veil was very beautiful and very costly. Made of finely-twisted linen fabric, the curtain shimmered with the colors of blue, purple, and scarlet.

The Lord instructed that this special veil was to be made under the supervision of those two outstanding craftsmen, Bezalel and Oholiab, men who were filled *with the Spirit of God in wisdom, in understanding, in knowledge, and in all kinds of craftsmanship* (Exodus 31:3). These skillful men were instructed to weave beautiful figures of cherubim into the fabric of the veil. Evidently the veil itself was very thick and heavy. This made certain that it would not be opened either by mistake or by any sudden gust of wind (Exodus 31:2-7).

The veil was held up by four pillars of acacia wood, each overlaid with gold. These pillars fit into silver bases. Their hooks were made of gold, and their sockets were made of silver. The veil itself was hung by clasps attached to the acacia wood frame. It was striking! (Exodus 26:31-33). Once the big veil was hung in place, then the Ark of the Covenant was brought into the Holy of Holies.

One purpose of the veil was to separate the Holy Place from the Holy of Holies. But even more importantly, it kept anyone from entering the Holy of Holies. Only the high priest was authorized to enter the Holy of Holies, there to be in the very presence of God Himself! And that happened only once each year!

On the Day of Atonement the high priest entered through the veil carrying the shed blood of a bull, taken from the altar of burnt offering. The high priest knew that if he entered at any other time, he would die. The ordinary Israelite could never enter the Holy of Holies, not even any of the other priests (Leviticus 16:2, 14).

In earlier days when the Lord first told Moses that He wanted the Israelites to build a sanctuary, the first piece of furniture for which He gave plans and measurements was the Ark of the Covenant.

The Lord indicated that the Ark, shaped like a chest, was to be made of acacia wood. But it was very important that the wood itself was to be overlaid with pure gold, both inside and outside. A golden molding was to be placed completely around it.

Four gold rings were to be cast. Two of the rings were to be fastened on one side of the Ark of the Covenant, and two rings were fastened on the other side of the Ark. Also, poles were to be made from acacia wood, each with an overlay of gold. These were then placed as carrying poles, one on each side of the ark, through the gold rings. The poles were never to be removed from the rings. They were left there permanently (Exodus 25:10-15).

All of this was very important. As the Israelites marched to the Promised Land, they had to be prepared to leave on their journey at a moment's notice. Since the Levites were the ones to carry the Ark, the poles permitted them to carry the Ark of the Covenant without touching it, which was forbidden.

Then there was the mercy seat. It was actually the cover for the Ark, placed on top of the Ark of the Covenant.

The Lord gave Moses the exact measurements for the construction of the mercy seat. The two cherubim and the mercy seat itself, were to be hammered out of one solid piece of gold. The cherubim were to be placed on either end of the mercy seat. They were to face each other. Their wings were to spread upward, covering the mercy seat. Their faces were to be turned toward the mercy seat. Above the mercy seat and between their arched wings was the actual place where God's glorious presence would manifest Himself to Israel.

This was the very spot that the Lord had talked about when He told Moses, *There I will meet with you; and from above the mercy seat, from between the two cherubim which are upon the ark of the testimony, I will speak to you about all that I will give you in commandment for the sons of Israel* (Exodus 25:22). And we know that God kept that promise throughout all the years of their wilderness journeys. It was there, at the mercy seat, where God was always present with His people.

Other instructions followed. The Lord also told Moses to put certain items in the Ark. There he was to place the tablets of the Ten Commandments (Deuteronomy 10:5). They had been given by the Lord as a reminder to the Israelites of God's faithful covenant and of the laws that they needed to follow.

A golden jar with manna was also put within the ark (Exodus 16:33-34). God miraculously preserved some of the manna to remind His people how He had fed them for forty years in the wilderness.

Likewise, Aaron's rod was placed in the ark (Numbers 17:10). That rod, which had miraculously budded and borne fruit, was proof that God had specifically chosen Aaron to be the high priest. It is very interesting that these same details are also mentioned in Hebrews 9:4 in the New Testament.

As God's chosen high priest, on the Day of Atonement, Aaron had to perform very important rituals for the forgiveness of the sins of the people of Israel. What were some of those rituals?

First, Aaron had to prepare himself by washing at the laver which stood in the courtyard in front of the tabernacle. After he was cleansed, he then entered the tabernacle and dressed in specially-prepared holy garments.

Aaron then slaughtered a bull, making atonement for his own sins as well as for those of his household. Taking a fire pan full of burning coals from the altar and two handfuls of sweet incense, Aaron next went through the veil into the Holy of Holies. There he placed the incense on the fire of the coals in the fire pan which he was carrying. This fire caused a cloud of incense to cover the mercy seat, where God's presence dwelt. Next, Aaron took the blood from the slaughtered bull and with his finger he sprinkled some of the blood of the sacrificed bull seven times on the east side of the mercy seat and seven times in front of the mercy seat (Leviticus 16:6,11,14).

Another Day of Atonement ritual involved two male goats. As the goats stood before Aaron at the doorway of the tent of meeting, he cast lots to determine which goat was to be sacrificed as a sin offering for the people. That goat was then slaughtered (Leviticus 16:5-10, 15). Its blood was brought through the veil into the Holy of Holies and sprinkled on the mercy seat and in front of the mercy seat, just as the bull's blood had been sprinkled there earlier.

When Aaron finished the atonement of the Holy Place, of the tent of meeting, and of the brazen altar, he then laid both of his hands on the head of the other goat.

As he did so, Aaron confessed over the head of the living goat all of the iniquities, all of the transgressions, and all of the sins of the sons of Israel. This was a transfer of the Israelites' guilt to the living goat. That goat would now bear away all of their many sins. Next, Aaron released that living goat and sent it away into the wild thickets to struggle and wander about in the barren wilderness (Leviticus 16:20-22).

And so what we see in all this is that for the Israelites, in their day, it was the shedding of the blood of sacrificed animals that brought them forgiveness of their sins. Year after year they were agonized by the knowledge of their sins and with their need for forgiveness. There were also many other rituals and ceremonies which Aaron, as well as the people, had to fulfill in order for them to be cleansed of their sins. These same rituals had to be repeated over and over again.

Now we know that all of those rituals have been forever fulfilled through the great atoning death of Christ upon the cross. When Jesus died on the cross, He became the ultimate sacrifice for our sins!

We now understand that it was not the shedding of the blood of mere bulls and goats that actually reconciled God and man in the days of the Old Testament. No! Hebrews 10:4 tells us, *For it is impossible for the blood of bulls and goats to take away sins.* They were merely symbols of that one great coming sacrifice of Jesus Christ, the Son of God, at Calvary. That sacrifice changed everything!

Indeed, at the very moment when Jesus died on the cross for our sins, the veil in the Jewish temple in Jerusalem, which separated the Holy Place from the Holy of Holies, was torn in two. God's Word tells us, *And Jesus cried out again with a loud voice, and yielded up His spirit. And behold, the veil of the temple was torn in two from top to bottom; and the earth shook and the rocks were split* (Matthew 27:50-51).

No human hand could have ever torn that veil from the top to the bottom. It was truly a miracle.

What does all of this mean to us today? It means that when we repent, and when we receive Christ as our Savior, our sins are forgiven. Christ is our great and ultimate Sacrifice!

Through the shedding of His blood at Calvary, now we have access to God's holy presence. The veil is gone. There is nothing to stop us. The way has been opened for us to go to Him directly and to enter into the glorious presence of our precious Lord and Savior.

We enter into God's presence through our prayers! As His children, we have the privilege of going to Him in prayer at any time. We can commune with Him day or night, at home, in school, or even as we work. He is right there by our side. He longs to have fellowship with us because we are His beloved daughters and sons. In Ephesians 6:18 we are encouraged to pray. *With all prayer and petition pray at all times in the Spirit, and with this in view, be on the alert with all perseverance and petition for all the saints.*

In God's presence we find peace and joy! The realization that we are living in His presence, fills our hearts with deep peace and overflowing joy. Together with the Psalmist we can say, *Let us come before His presence with thanksgiving, let us shout joyfully to Him with psalms* (Psalm 95:2). There is nothing more wonderful than to know that our Heavenly Father loves us. It is so important that we practice His presence and tell Him that we love Him also.

In God's presence we find many blessings! In Proverbs 28:20 it says, *A faithful man will abound with blessings.* This is so true. God continually pours out His blessings upon His children as we walk by His side. When we practice the presence of the Lord, He sends us blessings upon blessings upon blessings. Then our faith in Him is strengthened. We can place our entire future in His hands. We know that our Heavenly Father will be by our side until He calls us to be with Him forever in His eternal home.

In God's presence we find comfort in times of trials and heartache! I saw a wonderful example of this in the lives of a missionary family who lived in the same apartment complex as we did in Quito, Ecuador. John and Gloria Mosiman were wonderful neighbors. Our families celebrated Christmas and birthdays together. Many times our friend John and my husband Jack traveled together to neighboring Ecuadorian towns and cities to hold special Spanish evangelistic services.

Years later, after both of our families had returned to America, we continued our friendship by correspondence. One day we were deeply saddened to hear that John had developed a very rare type of cancer in his blood. He would receive chemotherapy, but the doctors had told John there was no cure for the type of cancer that he had.

We began to pray for him. Several months later he wrote to say that he was getting weaker. His cancer was advancing. However, his letter was a beautiful testimony.

As a child of God, John knew that at the moment of his death, he would enter everlasting life with His Lord. But already his heart was bursting with joy and thanksgiving to God! He knew that even now the Lord's presence was surrounding him constantly. He could feel His nearness and love. He knew that God was by his side and that God saw his cancer. He found strength as He prayed and communed with his Lord. While he rested in his bed, He felt His nearness and comfort.

During those months of illness, several young men came to visit him. As they sat by his bedside, John would challenge them to live for Christ. These young men were coming to encourage a dying man. But, rather, John would tell them of the great peace and joy that he continued to experience in Christ.

John was dying, but his testimony was all about joyfully living close to the Lord. These young men saw in John a true testimony of what it means to live in the fellowship and presence of the Lord without being overwhelmed by circumstances. They saw the contentment and close relationship that John had with His Savior, even while his body was suffering from cancer.

In John's last letter to me he talked about how blessed he was to feel God's presence. His closing words were, "I want to finish my life well." A short time later, John did just that. Today he is experiencing the Lord's heavenly presence in God's eternal home, HEAVEN. How wonderful that God's presence can give us special strength and encouragement in the midst of pain and suffering.

All through Scripture we see that God is everywhere, which means that His presence always surrounds us. Isn't it wonderful that *The eyes of the Lord move to and fro throughout the earth that He may strongly support those whose heart is completely His* (II Chronicles 16:9). This picture gives me great joy as we remember that the eyes of the Lord are upon each one of His children! Yes, He is everywhere!

The Lord invites us to come to Him. In Hebrews 4:16 He tells us, *Therefore let us draw near with confidence to the throne of grace, so that we may receive mercy and find grace to help in time of need.* We are His children! He is our Heavenly Father!

It is good to desire to grow spiritually. We are encouraged to "draw near with confidence to the throne of grace." What a blessing it is to constantly practice the presence of the Lord. How good it is to hear our Savior say, *Abide in Me, and I in you* (John 15:4). It is so wonderful to continually abide in the PRESENCE of our Lord!

Chapter 12

Our Heavenly Home

Many winters have passed since I first began to hear petitions from dear Slavic women for a book about how to grow spiritually. Many months have passed since I accepted their challenge and began to write such a book.

In this book we have used the tabernacle and its furnishings to illustrate practices and truths which will help us to grow spiritually. Do we remember those illustrations? Let us look at them once more.

First of all, we remember that there was only one entrance to the courtyard of the tabernacle. Likewise, Jesus tells us, *I am the door; if anyone enters through Me, he will be saved* (John 10:9).

We must make our decision. Do we continue in our sins outside of the gate? Or do we accept Christ's invitation to come through the open door of salvation? We must open our hearts to Jesus and enter through that door. This will lead us into the arms of Jesus. This is the first step towards growing spiritually.

Beyond the gate stood the brazen altar. On that altar animals were continually sacrificed to atone for men's sins.

However, for us today, we look to Calvary for our atonement. It was on Calvary's cross that Jesus suffered, shedding His blood for lost sinners. There by His death He paid for the sins of all mankind. When we repent of our sins, He cleanses us. When we accept Him into our hearts, we become children of our Heavenly Father. As His children, we will live with Him for all eternity in His Heavenly Home.

Beyond the brazen altar and near the entrance to the Holy Place, stood the laver. The laver was a container of water used by the priests for cleansing. The priests were required to wash all impurities from their hands and their feet each time they entered the Holy Place. They were to be clean before the Lord.

We, too, live in a dark and dirty world. How often our Christian testimony can become clogged with unkind words, unworthy thoughts, or evil actions. This does not please God. Whenever His Word convicts us of sin in our lives, we must ask God to cleanse us and to forgive us. We must strive for holiness. As we do this with a sincere heart, we will continue to grow spiritually.

As the priests entered the Holy Place, on their right stood the table of the Bread of the Presence. There the priests were nourished as they ate of the twelve fresh loaves of bread. For us, today, the Bread of the Presence on the table speaks of Christ as the Bread of Life. We are nourished as we daily read His Word. From it we receive strength to resist temptation. His Word teaches us truths that help us to grow spiritually and to become mature believers.

Earlier, we saw that across from the table of the Bread of the Presence stood the golden lampstand giving out its light. It was the only source of light in the dark tent of meeting.

In John 8:12 Jesus said, *I am the Light of the world; he who follows Me will not walk in the darkness but will have the Light of life.* Jesus is our only source of Eternal Light. The path of life is often dark, but the light of Jesus has brought hope into this sinful world.

Jesus also tells His followers, *You are the light of the world* (Matthew 5:14). This means that we must live in such a way that we reflect His glorious light. People are far more impressed by what we are and by what they see in us, than by what we may say. Most people will only see Jesus by seeing Him through us. How brightly are we shining?

We must take His message of salvation and share it with others. As we do this, our own hearts will glow brighter, and we will draw closer to Him.

The altar of incense stood in the center of the Holy Place, near the veil.

Surely the most noticeable thing about that golden altar was the overwhelming fragrance that rose upward from it. That perpetual sweet aroma was a symbol of worship and adoration. With this ritual, the Hebrew nation gave praise and thanksgiving to Jehovah.

The altar of incense is a good illustration for us today. Our prayers are like incense rising to heaven. Prayer is communicating with the Lord. When we pray we are drawn into oneness with Him. The Lord waits for us to speak to Him. "Call unto Me." He says.

We must go to Him in faith and ask Him for guidance and for wisdom. As we practice His presence, it is good to praise Him and thank Him for every blessing.

Prayer releases God's power. How many times I heard my father repeat, "Much prayer, much power."

And he truly lived by that conviction. As we devote ourselves to much prayer, the Lord will strengthen our spiritual life and will help us to grow in Him.

As we devote ourselves to much prayer, the Lord will strengthen our spiritual life and will help us to grow in Him.

We remember that a veil separated the Holy of Holies from the Holy Place. That veil kept people from entering the Holy of Holies. Only the high priest was permitted to part the veil and to enter once a year into the Holy of Holies where God dwelt.

Praise God, when Jesus died on the cross, that veil was torn from top to bottom! Now the way was open for His children to enter freely into the presence of our Lord. Today, those of us who are saved by His grace are blessed to be able to dwell in His presence with complete confidence. What a marvelous place to be: to live in the very presence of God! (Mark 15:38).

Almost every chapter of this book has shown us the steps that we need to take in order to grow spiritually. First of all, we have learned that we cannot live holy lives in our own strength.

We must pray! It is good to pray when we awake, and it is good to pray when we go to sleep! Indeed, our hearts must be in constant communion with our Lord throughout the entire day.

We must read His Word! The Lord speaks to us as we read His Holy Word. The Bible teaches us. It convicts us. It encourages us, and it gives us hope of eternal life with our Savior.

We must love the Lord with all our heart, soul, and strength. How blessed is the man whose strength is in the Lord! *They go from strength to strength* (Psalm 84:7).

Doing these things, we will grow spiritually! *But grow in the grace and knowledge of our Lord and Savior Jesus Christ* (II Peter 3:18).

The more we practice the presence of our Lord, the more closely we will be drawn to Him. The more we make Jesus the center of our lives and lean upon Him, the more we will realize that our inner spiritual man needs to be continually renewed.

As our spiritual man is renewed, we will no longer think only about ourselves. Our spirit will rise above all the fears and disappointments that we have harbored. This continual renewal is a wonderful preparation for that day when our Savior will take us out of this world to live with Him in our Heavenly Home.

So often we look longingly at the earthly things which surround us. Instead, let us fix our eyes on those things which are of eternal value. His Word tells us, *Set your mind on things above, not on the things that are on earth* (Colossians 3:2). It is time to think of our Heavenly Home.

Scripture refers to us who are believers as "aliens and strangers" on this earth. *For here* [on earth] *we do not have a lasting city,* says Hebrews 13:14, *but we are seeking the city which is to come.* Our days on earth are so temporal. We need to remember that this earth is NOT our forever home. We will take nothing with us when we leave this sinful world.

Let me explain. I heard of the death of a very prominent rich man. People spoke of the great wealth he had accumulated. Then they mentioned all the great things he had accomplished during his life. Suddenly, someone asked? "I wonder how much he left?" There was a pause. Then another voice was heard to say, "He left it ALL!" He took none of his great wealth into eternity.

Scripture tells us, *For our citizenship is in heaven, from which also we eagerly wait for a Savior, the Lord Jesus Christ* (Philippians 3:20). As a child of God, our true citizenship and our eternal home will be in Heaven someday!

During our days on earth we have the joy of practicing God's presence. We can feel His love. As we talk to Him we find great comfort in His fellowship. He is constantly by our side. But what brings us our greatest joy is that Jesus promises, *I will...receive you to Myself, that where I am, there you may be also* (John 14:3). So we have the assurance that one day, when it is His appointed time, our Heavenly Father will take us to His home in Heaven. There we will live with Christ forever!

What do we know about Heaven?

It was Jesus Himself who gave us one of the most vivid descriptions of Heaven. Jesus was telling His disciples, (as well as all of us who have repented of our sins), that He was going to His Father's House. He was going to Heaven! And there in His Father's Heavenly Home, Jesus was going to prepare a place for all of us in which to live forever. He made it very clear that in His Father's eternal home there will be many dwelling places with sufficient rooms for all of us. There are many people on this earth today that do not have their own home or even a place to live. But in John 14:1-3 we read where Jesus tells us that He, personally, is preparing a place for us to live in Heaven.

What will Heaven be like?

For one thing, there will be a great host of angels in Heaven. They are His messengers. Remember when the angel announced the birth of Jesus to the shepherds near Bethlehem? After that declaration, the angel was joined by a multitude of the heavenly host. This great choir of angels began praising God as they sang, *Glory to God in the highest, and on earth peace among men with whom He is pleased* (Luke 2:14). And, *there is joy in the presence of the angels of God over one sinner who repents* (Luke 15:10).

Who will be in Heaven?

The Bible tells us that in Heaven there will be multitudes of people who were purchased by the blood of Jesus. They will have come from every tribe, from every nation, and from every language of the world. They will be those who found salvation in Christ through the testimony of a multitude of pastors, missionaries, and faithful believers.

Some of these witnesses died in prisons. Others were martyred. Indeed, across the centuries, many have suffered for Christ. But in Heaven, God's ultimate blessing for all believers is that we will see Him face to face. We will be in His glorious presence for ever and ever--for all eternity (Revelation 5:9).

What will not be found in Heaven?

There will be no night in Heaven. No lamp light will be needed, nor the light of the sun, nor the light of the moon. This is because the glory of God has illuminated it, and its lamp is the Lamb (Jesus) (Revelation 21:23, 22:5).

There will be no death in Heaven. There will be no mourning, or crying, or pain. God will wipe away every tear from our eyes (Revelation 21:4). There will only be the joy of the Lord!

There will be nothing unclean in Heaven. We know that Heaven is a holy place! No one who practices abomination and lying will be allowed to enter Heaven (Revelation 21:27). Who are those who will enter Heaven?

Only those whose names are found written in the Lamb's book of Life will be allowed to enter Heaven. This is eternity's great record book. The name of every person who has repented and has asked Jesus to come into his heart is immediately written into the Lamb's book of Life (Revelation 21:27).

Let me tell you how my own dear Babushka, Anastasia Deyneka, entered heaven. In the first paragraph of this book I described the house in Belarus where my father was born. Well, Babushka continued living in that same yellow house in the village of Staramlynia for the rest of her life.

In chapter one I also described the moment when she accepted the Lord as her personal Savior. That was a glorious experience which brought peace and joy to her heart.

Babushka began to lose her eyesight at about ninety-five years of age. Both her daughter-in-law and her granddaughter Nastia lived with her and cared for her in the yellow house. By the time she reached her one hundredth birthday, she was spending much of her time in bed. One evening, soon after she celebrated that birthday, the family realized Babushka was suddenly failing. "We need to get someone," shouted her daughter-in-law. "Who can come? Whom should we call?" she exclaimed!

Just then, Babushka sat up straight in her bed. In a clear voice she said, "Don't call anyone. Stop fussing about me. I don't need anybody to help me. Jesus is calling me. I am going to Heaven."

With those strong, clear words ringing out, my one hundred year old Babushka Anastasia fell back on her bed and went to live in her Heavenly Home!

When we get to Heaven,
What a joy that will be.
When we see Jesus,
We will thank Him for Calvary.

When we get to Heaven,
Our joy will be complete.
We will spend all eternity
In our Father's Heavenly Home!

Epilogue

It was May 13, 2012. Sixteen years had passed since my first visit to the old House of Prayer in Dragichin, Belarus. This was the church which my Mama had often attended in her late teens. During 1925-1926 my Papa had preached there as well. Now in its place stood an imposing newly-built red brick building: THE DEYNEKA MEMORIAL CHURCH!

A service was being held to dedicate this new House of Prayer. It was also to commemorate the ministries of my father, Peter Naumovich Deyneka, Sr., founder of Slavic Gospel Association, and my brother, Peter Petrovich Deyneka, Jr., who founded Mission Eurasia.

Upon entering the church hall with my dear widowed sister-in-law, Anita Deyneka, the first thing we saw was a huge banner across the entire front of the church. It said, "MUCH PRAYER ~ MUCH POWER! My Papa would have loved it!

Beautiful, melodious Russian hymns were sung. Poetry was read. Anita and I gave greetings, as also did several visiting pastors. My cousin Nicolai Pavlovich Leonovich brought the closing message. This was followed by a prayer of dedication. Many expressed their gratefulness to God for this new House of Prayer.

Beside the church a log museum had been set up. It featured many family and ministry photographs and other exhibits of the past.

My heart was deeply touched by all we were experiencing. As our car pulled away, I wanted to engrave the vision of that House of Prayer on my heart forever. Yes, the building was only constructed of red bricks with a wooden floor.

But to me it stood as a glorious lighthouse proclaiming God's love in that region of the land of my heritage, Belarus!

A Visit to Staramlynia

The day following the House of Prayer dedication in Dragichin, we went to visit my Papa's village of Staramlynia. My heart beat faster as I anticipated seeing my Papa's old home once more. However, when the car stopped in front of the house, I was shocked!

The white picket fence was gone! The yellow paint of the boards of the house had faded. I got out and walked quickly to the entrance way. There was a big padlock on the closed door. Grass and wild flowers were growing in the patio. The house was abandoned. My cousin Nastia had died.

A piece of the roof was loose and hanging down. Bushes and trees were beginning to cover the windows. Pushing aside the branches, I peeked inside. There was only the dark, empty room, except for Babushka's table cloth still covering the simple table.

The gardens had gone wild. Only a few stray horse-radish leaves were peeking through the weeds.

I quickly went to see the well. It was covered over now. I pushed its cover aside and looked into it. Seeing that

there was still water down there, I gently replaced the cover.

Tears flowed as I stood and looked at my Babushka's deserted home. Oh, the stories it could tell! And, oh, the secrets and the dreams that are hidden there forever. Sadness came over me, both for the past and for the future. At that moment I knew I would never stand here again. Was this the end of the story?

No! Suddenly my heart cried out to the Lord with joy. Praise God for those who found the Lord in this house and in this village. There is the wonderful promise we have in

God's Word which says, *For we know that if the earthly tent which is our house is torn down, we have a building from God, a house not made with hands, eternal in the heavens* (II Corinthians 5:1).

Yes, I think about Heaven! I often think about Heaven! Several members of my immediate family are already enjoying their beautiful eternal home. Babushka was first, then my Papa, my Mama, my brother Peter, and not long ago my sister Lydia also joined them there.

How glorious to know that all those who trust Christ have the blessed hope of eternal life. I trust that you, too, will be joining me in our Father's Heavenly Home!

The Deynekas in 1947, during Ruth's college years
(Lydia, Peter and Ruth in back)

Ruth finds cousin Anastacia harvesting potatoes in
Staramlynia, September 1995.

Ladies eagerly gathered to hear Ruth
in the town of Rahachov, Belarus.

Ruth sharing the Gospel during tea
with a group of unchurched women in Lvov.

*The Baptist church in Omsk, now restored for worship
after being used as a courthouse and jail during the communist era.*

*Ruth urging cousin Anastacia to accept Christ,
winter 1996.*